SUPER SMART SCIENCE

SUPER SMART SCIENCE

Colleen Kessler

PRUFROCK PRESS INC.
WACO, TEXAS

Library of Congress Cataloging-in-Publication Data

Kessler, Colleen.
    Super smart science : 180 days of warm-ups and challenging activities / Colleen Kessler.
        p. cm.
    ISBN-13: 978-1-59363-213-7 (pbk.)
    ISBN-10: 1-59363-213-4
    1. Science—Study and teaching (Secondary)—Activity programs. 2. Science—Study and teaching (Elementary)—Activity programs. I. Title.
    LB1585.K472 2007
    507.1—dc22
                                2007008739

Edited by Jennifer Robins
Production Design by Marjorie Parker

ISBN-13: 978-1-59363-213-7
ISBN-10: 1-59363-213-4

Prufrock Press Inc.
P.O. Box 8813
Waco, TX 76714-8813
Phone: (800) 998-2208
Fax: (800) 240-0333
http://www.prufrock.com

Acknowledgements

Thank you to all the wonderful science teachers I ever had—and to those I didn't. Continue stoking the flame of inquiry in your students and watching wonder unfurl on their faces.

Thank you Brian, Trevor, Laura, Mom, and Dad for your understanding and encouragement during this project—how many of these teasers can you solve?

Introduction

Getting kids into the right frame of mind to think critically and flexibly is essential in any classroom, but I think it is especially important in the science classroom. Students need to study science with open, flexible, and seeking minds. They need to be ready to accept the unexpected.

This book is designed to exercise that flexibility and enhance your students' critical thinking for a few minutes each day, preparing them for and leaving them more open to the learning you have planned for them. Because most school districts follow a 180-day school year, this book contains 180 days of challenges—all based on national science standards. Although this book is not expected to follow along with your specific topic and lesson for the day, it does contain activities and teasers that should encourage your students' curiosity and make them feel challenged.

Some activities may stretch over a few days; this is indicated by the heading at the top of the page. There are three components to each "day": a Thought for the Day, a Cool Fact, and an Activity or Teaser to attempt. As you complete the activities and teasers in this book, please remind your students that they should not attempt any of these without a parent or teacher helping them for reasons of safety.

The Thought for the Day is a quote related to the field of science. Use this to get students thinking. Ask for their interpretations or thoughts regarding what was said. Don't spend too much time on this—your students don't need to delve into the hidden depths of the quotation at this time. This is just a quick chance to let them think a little. Some interesting discussions may arise when a quote touches students; you may witness some interesting debates, giving you wonderful insight into the way your students think. When this does occur, it is often worth the extra few minutes the spontaneous discussion takes away from regular class time.

The Cool Fact is usually related to the Activity or Teaser and is a bit of trivia—something most students like to learn. Challenge your students to solve the Activity or Teaser (see below) first, and then post or share the Cool Fact to further their understanding of what they've just learned. Write it on the board or read it to them, and challenge them to slip it into conversation with their parents or siblings to try to stump them.

The Activity or Teaser, depending on the day, is a short experiment, brain teaser, or critical-thinking puzzler designed to get your students thinking. Some activities may take a few minutes of your time over the course of a few days. Have the experiment set up and use it as a hook for the day to get your students interested in working. The Teaser is a fun challenge to set up with students. Post it at the beginning of the class period and allow students to try and guess what the answer is, revealing it at the end of class or the next day if nobody has solved it yet. Or, you could have your students ask you "yes" and "no" questions, trying to narrow down the focus until they arrive at the correct solution.

All of these are suggestions for using the challenges in this book. The best use will come, though, if you make it your own. Figure out how these "hooks" fit best into your day and the structure of your classroom. But, use them! You'll be surprised at how excited your students will be about the learning that is taking place.

Day 1

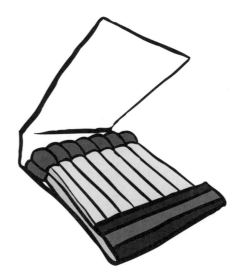

Thought for the Day

Give me a lever long enough and a fulcrum on which to place it, and I shall move the world.
—Archimedes

Cool Fact

One type of beetle, the Melanophila, actually seeks out fire, while most organisms flee from burning areas. The beetle uses special sensory organs to search out wavelengths of infrared light consistent with burning wood so it can lay its eggs in the newly charred pieces.

Teaser

Jenny had a small glass, a match, a lemon wedge, and a plate. She poured enough water on the plate to cover the bottom. She told her friend that she could get the water in the glass without touching or moving the plate. Her friend said that it was impossible. Jenny was right. She was able to get the water in the glass using only the materials she had. How did she do it?

Solution

The first thing she did was stick the match in the lemon wedge to make it stand up straight. Then, she set the lemon wedge in the middle of the plate, lit the match, and set the glass upside down over the lit match. The flame "eats" the oxygen in the glass, creating a vacuum that sucks the water through the space between the glass and the plate, pulling the water up into the glass.

Day2

Thought for the Day

Aerodynamically, the bumble bee shouldn't be able to fly, but the bumble bee doesn't know it so it goes on flying anyway.
—Mary Kay Ash

Cool Fact

The Transmission Electron Microscope, which was developed in 1931 by Max Knoll and Ernst Ruska, was similar to the Light Transmission Microscope, but focused a beam of electrons (instead of light) through the object it was magnifying.

Teaser

Dr. Nick was using his laboratory's new high-powered scanning electron microscope to view a slide he had prepared of a bumblebee. He looked at the monitor and saw a bright yellow bumblebee clinging to a leaf just like the slide he had prepared. However, Dr. Nick was sure someone was playing a trick on him. He checked the cables, and sure enough, the microscope was not hooked up.

How did Dr. Nick know he was being tricked?

Solution

The bumblebee image appeared in color, which electron microscopes cannot show. Only light microscopes show color.

Day 3

Thought for the Day

There is a single light of science, and to brighten it anywhere is to brighten it everywhere.
—Isaac Asimov

Cool Fact

Sunburn is a visible reaction to the sun's invisible ultraviolet rays. Ultraviolet radiation can also cause invisible damage to the skin. In fact, skin cancer is the most common kind of cancer in the United States and exposure to the sun is the No. 1 cause for skin cancer.

Teaser

Joanna doesn't like to spend a lot of time outside on sunny days. She doesn't want to get sunburned because she has heard how it contributes to skin cancer. One cloudy day, her friends convinced her to go to the park for a picnic. They played by the lake all day. When she got home that evening, Joanna looked in the mirror and realized that she had gotten the worst sunburn of her life! How was it possible that she had gotten badly burnt on such a cloudy day?

Solution

Although most of the sunlight isn't able to penetrate the cloud cover, the harmful UV rays that cause skin cancer and burn your skin still go through the clouds

Day 4

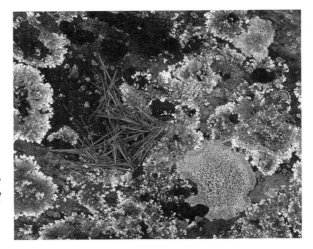

Thought for the Day

Nothing has such power to broaden the mind as the ability to investigate systematically and truly all that comes under thy observation in life.
—Marcus Aurelius

Cool Fact

Mold spores are not able to grow if moisture is not present.

Teaser

This begins as a single-celled organism, feeding on whatever is nearby, then as food becomes scarce, joins with other single-celled "brothers" to form a multicellular animal-like organism that moves to a better location. Once there, it becomes a plant and grows many small black spores, releasing them to reproduce. What is it?

Solution

Slime mold. This begins as a single-celled organism, getting together with more slime mold and forming a multicellular organism called a pseudoplasmodium that is capable of slug-like movement. When it reaches a better location, it grows a stalk and produces black mold spores. It releases the spores one at a time, which starts the process all over again.

Day 5

Thought for the Day

Your theory is crazy, but it's not crazy enough to be true.
—Niels Bohr

Cool Fact

In July 1985, Coca-Cola was the first soft drink enjoyed in outer space on the Space Shuttle Challenger. A special space can was developed.

Teaser

Harrison was sucking on a candy-coated mint when he saw Tom drinking a Coke. He told Tom that he could make the Coke he was drinking erupt like a volcano. Tom didn't believe him, but he handed him the Coke anyway. Harrison spit the mint into the Coke and Tom jumped back—he was surprised to see that Harrison was right. The Coke was now frothing and bubbling like an aluminum-can volcano. How did this happen?

Solution

Spitting the mint into the Coke breaks the surface tension, making new bubbles form easily. Then, there is a reaction (similar to that of baking soda and vinegar) between the ingredients in the mint and the Coke.

Day 6

Thought for the Day

Touch a scientist and you touch a child.
—Ray Bradbury

Cool Fact

Venus has more volcanoes than any other planet in our solar system. There are more than 1,600 known volcanoes on Venus, but scientists estimate that there may be as many as 100,000 that haven't been counted yet. None seem currently active, but scientists can't be completely sure.

Teaser

One of the most popular activities in any science fair is the baking soda volcano. The Moreland Hills School Science Fair was no different. Two students set up their clay volcanoes next to each other and gathered the exact same ingredients: baking soda and vinegar. Ellie and Allie both began adding ingredients into their volcanoes at the same time. Within seconds, Ellie's volcano began spewing lava all over the table and floor. Allie's volcano did very little. Considering that they used the exact same amounts of the exact same materials, why didn't Allie's work as well as Ellie's?

Solution

Allie put the vinegar in first and then added the baking soda, whereas Ellie put the baking soda in first and poured the vinegar over it. Due to the type of reaction, Ellie's way makes a bigger "eruption" and mess!

Day 7

Thought for the Day

Research is what I'm doing when I don't know what I'm doing.
—Wernher von Braun

Cool Fact

Fresh water freezes at 0 degrees Celsius (32 degrees Fahrenheit), but seawater doesn't freeze until it reaches about negative 2 degrees Celsius because nearly 3% of it is made up of salt. This is why people living in cold climates put salt on the roads during the winter to prevent ice from forming.

Activity

Freezing Point

This activity demonstrates that salt lowers the freezing point of water, and that this ability makes it perfect for de-icing in the winter—or making homemade ice cream in the summer.

Materials (per student):
- 2 tablespoons sugar
- 1 cup half and half or whole milk
- ½ teaspoon vanilla extract
- ½ cup salt (bigger granules like rock or kosher salt work best, but table salt will work also)
- ice cubes (enough to almost fill the gallon-sized bag)
- 1 pint-sized zipper bag
- 1 gallon-sized zipper bag
- thermometer

Procedures:
1. Have students fill their gallon-sized bags half full with ice.
2. Ask them to place the thermometer in the bag and set it aside.
3. Have them put the sugar, milk, and vanilla in the small zipper bag and seal it, squeezing as much air out as possible.

4. Have students take the thermometer out of the first zipper bag, record the temperature, and add the salt to the ice.
5. Have them shake the ice and salt well to mix them, and put the thermometer back in the zipper bag for 3 minutes.
6. Have them record the temperature.
7. Tell your students to put the small zipper bag inside the large zipper bag and seal it. (Make sure *both* zipper bags are sealed completely.)
8. Have them shake the zipper bags for about 5–7 minutes as hard as they can.
9. Ask them to take the small bag out of the large bag and check the consistency of the milk mixture.
10. Discuss how sodium chloride lowers the freezing point of the ice, helping to change the physical consistency of the milk mixture into homemade ice cream. Let them eat their results!

Day 8

Thought for the Day

Science is wonderfully equipped to answer the question "How?" but it gets terribly confused when you ask the question "Why?"
—Erwin Chargaff

Cool Fact

Dr. John S. Pemberton invented Coca-Cola in 1886, although he only sold about 9 drinks a day. Today, Coca-Cola is consumed at a rate of more than one billion drinks a day in 200 countries.

Activity

Coke Floats

This activity will demonstrate the differing buoyancy of similar objects.

Materials (for teacher to use in demonstration):
- clear container of water
- unopened can of Coke
- unopened can of Diet Coke

Procedures:
1. Ask your students to predict what will happen when you drop the cans of soda into the container of water.
2. Place them both in the water and record student observations on the board.
3. Ask your students to discuss why they think that the Diet Coke floated and the regular Coke sank.
4. Discuss why the cans behaved this way. (The cans contain the same volume, but artificial sweetener weighs much less than sugar and the amount of sweetener used in diet drinks is much less in volume than the amount of sugar used in regular drinks. Therefore, diet drinks are less dense—and more buoyant—than regular drinks.)

Day 9

Thought for the Day

If an elderly but distinguished scientist says that something is possible, he is almost certainly right; but if he says that it is impossible, he is very probably wrong.
—Arthur C. Clarke

Cool Fact

In the 18th century, a scientist named Daniel Bernoulli discovered a scientific principle that now carries his name. It became the basis for airplane flight many years after its discovery. The Bernoulli principle states that the faster air flows, the less pressure it exerts.

Activity

Bubble Dynamics Part One

This activity demonstrates the Bernoulli principle of aerodynamics.

Materials:
* container
* 1 cup dishwashing liquid
* small containers
* straws
* index cards

Procedures:
1. Prepare the bubble solution by mixing one cup of dish-washing liquid with one gallon of water.
2. Separate the solution into several smaller containers and scatter around the room.
3. Explain Bernoulli's principle to your students (see the Cool Fact for today).
4. Scientists have discovered that regardless of whether the air goes over or under the wing, it arrives at the other side of

the wing at the same instant. Ask: What does the Bernoulli principle say about faster moving air?

5. Have the students blow bubbles and experiment with different ways of keeping their bubbles afloat. They could use their hands or you can provide them with index cards.

6. Talk about what your students observed as they kept their bubbles floating. What worked? What didn't? How can they apply this to Bernoulli's principle?

Day 10

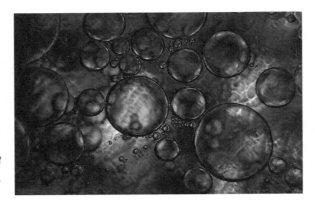

Thought for the Day

What is a scientist after all? It is a curious man looking through a keyhole, the keyhole of nature, trying to know what's going on.
—Jacques Cousteau

Cool Fact

The "skin" of a bubble is thin and stretchy, like rubber. When you blow a bubble and it floats away, the tension in the bubble skin tries to reduce the bubble into the shape with the smallest surface area possible for the amount of air it contains. The shape it always forms is a sphere.

Activity

Bubble Dynamics Part Two

This activity demonstrates the Bernoulli principle of aerodynamics.

Materials:
- container
- 1 cup dishwashing liquid
- small containers
- straws
- index cards

Procedures:
1. Prepare the bubble solution by mixing one cup of dishwashing liquid with one gallon of water.
2. Set up a "bubble obstacle course" that includes corners, curves, and hoops.
3. Remind your students of their experimentation the day before.
4. Have them use some of their strategies for keeping their bubble afloat and apply them to getting their bubble from one end of the obstacle course to the other safely.

Day 11

Thought for the Day

Nothing in life is to be feared. It is only to be understood.
—Marie Curie

Cool Fact

In 1803, Luke Howard invented the classification system we now use to describe different cloud types. He used Latin words that described what the clouds look like. We now use 10 different names to describe the clouds we see in the sky, all based on the original Latin words Howard used more than two centuries ago.

Activity

Clouds in a Bottle

This is a simple demonstration that shows the effects of pressure and temperature on cloud formation.

Materials (for teacher to use in demonstration):
- large, wide-mouthed glass jar (pickle jars, mayonnaise jars, and the like work well)
- thick plastic bag
- rubber bands
- water
- match

Procedures:
1. Fill the jar about ¼ of the way with water.
2. Place a lit match in the jar and quickly put the clear plastic bag over the top and seal it tightly with a rubber band.
3. Ask your students to share their observations. (The smoke from the match should be disappearing.)
4. Then, push the top of the bag into the jar really quickly and pull it out.

5. Ask your students to describe what is happening now. (A white cloud should form inside the jar. Water droplets should also be forming on the walls of the jar.)

Day 12

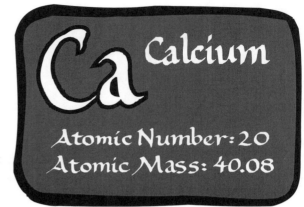

Thought for the Day

Every great advance in science has issued from a new audacity of imagination.
—John Dewey

Cool Fact

The periodic table was first created in 1869 by Dmitry I. Mendeleyev as a way to present all of the elements in order to show their similarities and differences.

Teaser

What one word do these three spell?
Calcium
Neodymium
Yttrium

Solution

Candy. (Check out the periodic table and the elements' abbreviations—Calcium: Ca; Neodymium: Nd; and Yttrium: Y.)

Day 13

Thought for the Day

No amount of experimentation can ever prove me right; a single experiment can prove me wrong.
—Albert Einstein

Cool Fact

The Earth weighs approximately 5.972 sextillion metric tons.

Teaser

I am a mother with a problem. Every day I gain tons, but never eat. How is this possible?

Solution

She is "Mother Earth." Every day, nearly 100 tons of dust and rock particles settle in the atmosphere and on her surface.

Day 14

Thought for the Day

Bad times have a scientific value. These are occasions a good learner would not miss.
—Ralph Waldo Emerson

Cool Fact

On March 28, 1910, the first successful seaplane take-off from water occurred in Martigues, France. Le Canard, as the seaplane was called, was flown by its inventor, Henri Fabre. The 50-horsepower rotary engine powered the plane an impressive 1,650-foot distance over water.

Teaser

No wheels came down when it was time to land the plane, yet the pilot was unconcerned and landed without a hitch. How was this possible?

Solution

The plane was a seaplane, which needs no wheels because it lands on water.

Day 15

Thought for the Day

The fewer the facts, the stronger the opinion.
—Arnold H. Glasow

Cool Fact

Extinction is a natural part of evolution because for some species to survive, others must die out. Since life began, about 99% of the Earth's species have disappeared and, on several occasions, huge numbers have died out in a relatively short time. The most recent of these mass extinctions, about 65 million years ago, swept away the dinosaurs and many other forms of life.

Teaser

The Tasmanian Wolf, a carnivorous marsupial and cousin to the wombat and kangaroo, does not eat meat, despite being classified as a carnivore. Why not?

Solution

It is extinct!

Day 16

Thought for the Day

From now on we live in a world where man has walked on the moon. It's not a miracle; we just decided to go.
—Tom Hanks in *Apollo 13*

Cool Fact

Cocoa trees produce pods, each containing approximately 20–50 cocoa beans. There are different varieties of cocoa beans used to make different kinds of chocolate. Cocoa beans must be fermented, dried, and roasted before being ground to make chocolate.

Teaser

What five chemical elements make chocolate?

Solution

Carbon (C)
Holmium (Ho)
Cobalt (Co)
Lanthanum (La)
Tellurium (Te)

Together they make chocolate (C Ho Co La Te).

Day 17

Thought for the Day

The great tragedy of science—the slaying of a beautiful hypothesis by an ugly fact.
—Thomas Huxley

Cool Fact

Water molecules are constantly cycling through the Earth. During the course of 100 years, a water molecule will spend about 98 years in the ocean, 20 months frozen, about 2 weeks in lakes and rivers, and less than a week in the atmosphere before starting the process over again.

Teaser

Water freezes from the top to the bottom, so if you left a glass of water in the freezer until only half of it was frozen, the bottom would still be liquid. What would happen if you started to freeze it when the glass was upside down?

Solution

Nothing. The water would pour out of the cup long before it would freeze.

Day 18

Thought for the Day

Anthropology demands the open-mindedness with which one must look and listen, record in astonishment and wonder that which one would not have been able to guess.
—Margaret Mead

Cool Fact

In 1979, American scientist Dr. Sylvia Earle made the world's deepest solo dive in a submersible to a depth of 380 meters (1,250 feet) off the Hawaiian coast using a diving suit called a "Jim Suit." Her record still stands.

Teaser

When oceanographers drop a heavy piece of equipment overboard to do their work in the water, does the water level change?

Solution

The equipment in the boat displaces an amount of water equal to the mass of the equipment. The equipment in the water displaces an amount of water equal to the volume of the equipment. Water is unable to support the level of salinity it would take to make it as dense as equipment, so the amount of water displaced by the boat is definitely more than the second amount, and the water level drops.

Days 19–20

Thought for the Day

Happiness hates the timid! So does science!
—Eugene O'Neill

Cool Fact

In 1994, Guy Nègre came up with the design for an air-powered car. By 2002, he had developed prototypes for two different types of engines: one designed for city use, where the driver wouldn't need to go more than 50 km/hour (approximately 31 mph), and the other a combination engine for out-of-city driving at faster speeds.

Activity

Puff Vehicles

This activity will allow students to observe cause and effect as they construct, test, and refine vehicles designed to move using only puffs of air.

Materials (per group) to use in building the vehicles:
- 10 straight, plastic straws
- 1 sheet of computer paper
- 4 wooden beads or spools
- 1 straight pin
- small baggies

Procedures:
1. Divide students into groups of three or four.
2. Have them take 2–3 minutes and brainstorm as a group what they could do with their materials to create a working vehicle.
3. Pass out the materials, making sure they've already been divided into the baggies.
4. Allow students 15 minutes to build and refine their designs.

5. Put the "cars" away until the following day.

6. The next day, go out with the groups into a long hallway where you have already marked a start and finish line.

7. Have each group choose its best "blower," who may use a straw or his or her mouth to blow, and time the vehicles from the start to the finish line.

8. Talk about which vehicles worked best and why. What would students do to improve their designs if they had another chance at this activity?

Day 21

Thought for the Day

Facts are the air of scientists. Without them you can never fly.
—Linus Pauling

Cool Fact

Just because air particles are invisible doesn't mean they don't weigh anything. In fact, they have weight and take up space. Air pressure is the weight of all those tiny particles pushing their weight on an object.

Teaser

Evie and Samantha were hanging out in the kitchen when Samantha told Evie that she could make a quarter jump up and down without touching it. Evie didn't believe it was possible, but she told Samantha to try. Samantha took an empty 2-liter bottle out of the freezer and placed a quarter on its mouth. The quarter began jumping. What was happening?

Solution

The cold air inside the bottle expanded when placed in a warmer location and was trying to escape the only way out—through the mouth of the bottle. Because the quarter was blocking it, the cool air moved the quarter enough so a little could escape.

Day 22

Thought for the Day

There is one thing even more vital to science than intelligent methods; and that is, the sincere desire to find out the truth, whatever it may be.
—Charles Pierce

Cool Fact

Many people have wondered over the years how planes at air shows can fly upside down. A simplified explanation is that aerobatic aircraft have specially shaped, symmetrical wings so the air is accelerated over both the top and bottom surfaces. This produces low pressure above and below the wing, so when the aircraft is inverted, the wings are still creating lift.

Teaser

A pilot is flying his bomber on a test run. Everything works perfectly. When he pushes the button to release the practice bomb, nothing happens. If everything is in working order, why didn't the bomb release?

Solution

He was flying upside down.

Day 23

Thought for the Day

The scientific theory I like best is that the rings of Saturn are composed entirely of lost airline luggage.
—Mark Russell

Cool Fact

An elephant's trunk is nothing more than an elongation of its nose and upper lip. It can be used for breathing and smelling, as well as for grabbing things. Elephants can pull up to 3 gallons of water into their trunk to be sprayed into their mouths for drinking or onto their backs for bathing. They also use two "fingers" that are at the tip of the trunk to pick up small things like grass or twigs.

Teaser

Why do elephants have such big ears? They have no predators and feed on plants, so they don't need to hear particularly well.

Solution

They're for regulating the elephant's body temperature. Because elephants have a large body mass compared to their skin surface, they need the extra skin surface provided by the ears to regulate their internal body temperature.

Day 24

Thought for the Day

Science is a way of thinking much more than it is a body of knowledge.
—Carl Sagan

Cool Fact

The word *salary* comes from the Latin word, *salarium*, which means "salt allowance" and was used in Roman times when workers were given money to buy salt.

Teaser

The freezing point of water is 32 degrees Fahrenheit. How is it possible to cool the water an additional 20 degrees and keep it in its liquid form?

Solution

Add salt. When you add salt to water, you lower water's freezing point. If you add enough, you can get it 20 degrees below its normal freezing level.

Day 25

Thought for the Day

A fact is a simple statement that everyone believes. It is innocent, unless found guilty. A hypothesis is a novel suggestion that no one wants to believe. It is guilty, until found effective.
—Edward Teller

Cool Fact

Erosion by running water is the most common form of erosion, although it takes place over a longer period of time than other forms. When water from rain or melted snow moves downhill, it can carry loose rock or soil with it. Erosion by running water forms the familiar gullies and V-shaped valleys that pepper most landscapes.

Activity

Weathering by Running Water

This activity will demonstrate what erosion caused by water running over stream beds or rocks would look like over time.

Materials:
- smooth river rock samples
- several sedimentary rock samples (with pointy edges) for each student or pair of students (limestone or sandstone will work best)
- plastic jars or bottles with screw-top lids (clean peanut butter jars work well) for each student or pair of students
- water
- timer

Procedures:
1. Compare the smooth river stones to the sharper-edge sedimentary rocks.
2. Ask for observations.
3. Have your students put three to four sedimentary rocks in their jars and fill to about an inch from the top with water.

4. Make sure the lids are all on tightly and have your students shake their jars vigorously for 2–4 minutes. (Put on some "rock" music and dance around the room!)
5. Let the water settle down and take out the rocks. What do the students notice? The edges should be a little smoother and there should be some rock particles in the water.
6. Explain that this is what happens when water runs along a stream bed or over rocks for long periods of time.

Days 26–28

Thought for the Day

In all science, error precedes the truth, and it is better it should go first than last.
—Hugh Walpole

Cool Fact

When water in rock cavities freezes and thaws repeatedly, it splits rock into small pieces because the water expands when it freezes.

Activity

Weathering by Freezing Water

This activity will demonstrate what erosion caused by freezing water would look like over time.

Note: This activity will take several days of observation.

Materials:
- large chunk of clay
- plastic baggie
- water
- freezer

Procedures:
1. Place a wet chunk of clay on a table and allow students to help form it into a large block or ball with a smooth surface.
2. Making sure it is still wet, have students watch you place it into a bag and put it into the cafeteria (or teacher's lounge) freezer.
3. Ask them to predict what will happen.
4. Leave it in overnight.
5. The next day, take it out and observe. What happened? (There should be some small cracks in the surface.) Why do the students think this occurred?

6. Wet it again (being careful not to disturb the newly formed cracks), and place it back into the bag and back into the freezer.
7. The next day, observe the cracks (they should be much wider) and measure them. Why do the students think this happened?
8. You could continue this for several more days, watching the cracks widen.
9. Discuss the changes that have occurred in the clay, comparing them to water freezing in the rocks along river banks and causing them to crack, rain freezing in roads and causing potholes and cracks along the sidewalk, and so forth.
10. This could also prompt a discussion about the changes in the states of matter (i.e., water expands when frozen).

Day 29

Thought for the Day

There is a single light of science, and to brighten it anywhere is to brighten it everywhere.
—Isaac Asimov

Cool Fact

Wind is an important cause of erosion only in dry regions because it can carry sand and dust, which can blemish even solid rock.

Activity

Weathering by Wind

This activity will demonstrate what erosion caused by wind blowing over rocks in the desert would look like over time.

Material (for each student or group):
- large pieces of sidewalk chalk
- cups
- white playground sand or salt
- wooden craft sticks

Procedures:
1. Determine whether you want students to work alone or in small groups.
2. Fill a cup halfway with salt or sand and a piece of sidewalk chalk.
3. Ask your students to stir the chalk through the sand with a wooden craft stick.
4. Discuss what happens (the sand becomes colored and the chalk wears away).

Day 30

Thought for the Day

OK, so what's the speed of dark?
—Steven Wright

Cool Fact

Isopropyl alcohol (rubbing alcohol) is commonly used as a sanitizer, cleaning agent, and a solvent. Most people have it in their homes.

Teaser

Ryan says he can burn a piece of paper without causing it any damage. How is this possible?

Solution

Ryan soaked the paper in 50% isopropyl alcohol. Thus, the alcohol burned, but the paper didn't.

Day 31

Thought for the Day

The important thing in science is not so much to obtain new facts as to discover new ways of thinking about them.
—Sir William Bragg

Cool Fact

The ironwood tree is only found in the Sonoran Desert. It is remarkably long-lived—growing up to 45 feet high and lasting more than 1,600 years.

Teaser

"I bet I can make this rock float and this piece of wood sink," said Ben.

"Impossible," disagreed Isabelle.

Ben dropped the rock and the wood in a container of water—the rock floated gently on the surface, while the wood sunk. How did Ben do it?

(The rock and wood were both real and occur naturally.)

Solution

The rock was pumice and the wood was a piece of the ironwood tree. Pumice is able to float because it lacks density. The ironwood is so dense it sinks in water.

Day 32

Thought for the Day

Science may set limits to knowledge, but should not set limits to imagination.
—Bertrand Russell

Cool Fact

Cubic zirconia is made from zirconium oxide powders evened out with magnesium and calcium.

Teaser

There were two candidates interviewing for the position of geology professor at Blake College. The head of the department believed one of them was lying about his credentials so he offered a test: He asked each to identify several pairs of rock and mineral samples. The candidates were able to identify each sample, but when the department head got to the last sample with the man he suspected of lying, the man told him that it was easy—they were both diamonds. The department head asked the man to leave, saying he had obviously never taken a geology course before and was certainly not qualified to teach the subject. How did the department head know?

Solution

The sample was of a diamond and a cubic zirconia. Anyone who had ever taken a geology class would have known the difference. Cubic zirconia is flawless and colorless, whereas most diamonds have some visible flaws and possess a yellowish tint.

Day 33

Thought for the Day

I maintain there is much more wonder in science than in pseudoscience. And in addition, to whatever measure this term has any meaning, science has the additional virtue, and it is not an inconsiderable one, of being true.
—Carl Sagan

Cool Fact

Heat causes expansion because it increases the vibrations of an object's atoms or molecules. In a gas, heat also increases the speed at which the atoms or molecules move. The increased movement forces the atoms or molecules farther apart and the body becomes larger.

Activity

Magical Balloons

This activity demonstrates the principles surrounding air expansion, as balloons inflate before your students' eyes.

Materials (for teacher to use in demonstration):
- 2-liter bottle
- bowl
- hot water
- cold water
- balloons

Procedures:
1. Fill the 2-liter bottle with really hot water.
2. Let this sit for a few minutes.
3. Fill the bowl with very cold water.
4. Empty the bottle into the sink (or another bowl).
5. Place the balloon over the lip of the bottle and place the bottle in the bowl of very cold water.
6. Ask your students to talk about what they observe. (The warm water heats the bottle. When the water is poured out,

the heated bottle then heats the air inside of it. When the bottle is placed in the cold water, the air inside the bottle cools and contracts [gets smaller and takes up less room], causing outside air to be drawn in, pulling the balloon in and inflating it inside the bottle.)

Days 34–35

Thought for the Day

There are in fact two things, science and opinion; the former begets knowledge, the latter ignorance.
—Hippocrates

Cool Fact

Transpiration is the process by which water is absorbed by plants, then evaporates into the atmosphere.

Activity

Water Loss

This activity demonstrates the act of transpiration.

Materials:
- a growing houseplant
- two clear plastic bags
- tape

Procedures:
1. Place one bag over a leaf on the houseplant and secure it on the stem with tape.
2. Fill the second bag with air (without blowing into it) and seal it around another leaf with tape.
3. Place both the bag and the plant in a sunny window and leave them there overnight.
4. The next day, have the students check both bags.
5. Discuss the results. (There should be water droplets on the inside of the bag that contained the air. There may be a little—but not much—water on the inside of the other bag as well.)

Day 36

Thought for the Day

I am among those who think that science has great beauty. A scientist in his laboratory is not only a technician: he is also a child placed before natural phenomena which impress him like a fairy tale.
—Marie Curie

Cool Fact

Atmospheric pressure is produced by the weight of the air from the top of the atmosphere as it presses down upon the layers of air below it.

Activity

Air Pressure

This activity uses common materials to demonstrate the effects of air pressure.

Materials (for teacher to use in demonstration):
- glass jar
- straw
- clay

Procedures:
1. Fill the jar with water.
2. Put the lid on the jar.
3. Poke a hole in the lid of the jar that is just big enough for the straw to poke through.
4. Place the straw in the hole.
5. Seal the hole very tightly with the clay.
6. Have a student try to suck the water out of the jar.
7. Have your students talk about what happened and why. (When you drink from a straw and cup, air pressure pushes down on the water, while the pressure inside your mouth is reduced because of the sucking. The outside air pressure forces the water up the straw. When the lid of the jar is sealed off, there is no outside air pressure to force the water up the straw.)

Day 37

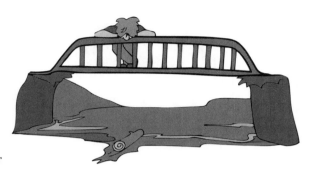

Thought for the Day

There is something fascinating about science. One gets such wholesome returns of conjecture out of such a trifling investment of fact.
—Mark Twain

Cool Fact

Early cantilever bridges were built in China and Tibet out of timber more than 1,900 years ago.

Teaser

A truck comes to a 1,000 ft.-long bridge and stops right before it to read a sign. The sign says that the maximum weight the bridge can hold is 4 tons, which is the exact weight of the truck. The truck proceeds on its way across the bridge. About halfway over the bridge a little bird lands on the top of the truck. Does the bridge break?

Solution

No, because by the time the truck is halfway across the bridge it has burned enough gas, which brings its weight down, to let the bird sit on it without the bridge breaking.

Day 38

Thought for the Day

In science the credit goes to the man who convinces the world, not the man to whom the idea first occurs.
—Sir Frances Darwin

Cool Fact

There are similarities and differences in the anatomy of dog breeds. All dogs have 27 bones from their nose to where their tail begins, but each breed has a different number of bones in its tail, depending on its length.

Activity

Bone Museum

This activity allows students to develop their observation skills as they compare bones from different species.

Materials:
*   whole chicken skeleton (follow the directions below)
*   human skeleton model
*   any other bones you can borrow (from local museums, high schools, or colleges)

Procedures:
1. Before presenting this activity to the class:
    *   Boil a chicken long enough for the meat to peel off easily.
    *   Clean the skeleton thoroughly (and carefully).
    *   Place the skeleton in the oven on a low temperature for several hours until completely dry.
2. Have your students help you identify and label key bones on the chicken and their purpose (femur, tibia, fibula, sternum, wishbone, vertebrae, ribs, etc.).
3. As a class, create museum labels for each bone, including information about the purpose it serves.

4. Display near the human and other skeletons for a hands-on museum experience in the classroom where students can compare the similarities and differences between human bone structure and that of other species.

Day 39

Thought for the Day

Equipped with his five senses, man explores the universe around him and calls the adventure Science.
—Edwin Powell Hubble

Cool Fact

Before conducting a dig, archaeologists do a survey of the area they are interested in excavating. Because excavations are expensive, archaeologists want to be sure they'll find something. A survey includes looking for mounds, foundations, and other visual structures, and collecting potsherds—which are broken pots. Archaeologists then draw maps and charts and take pictures of the area.

Activity

Dig In

This activity allows students to further their observation skills while using tools to excavate an archaeological dig.

Materials (enough for each student):
- cupcakes prepared beforehand according to the directions below
- small toys (party favors)
- toothpicks, toothbrushes, small paper towels, etc.
- paper plates

Procedures:
1. The night before this lesson, make cupcakes for your students.
   - Use a packaged mix
   - Fill each cupcake paper partway, insert one of the small toys, and cover with more cupcake mix. (Make sure the toy is completely covered.)
   - Bake according to directions, cool, and bring the cupcakes to school in the morning.

2. Give each student a cupcake, paper plate, and two toothpicks.
3. Have them carefully excavate their toy from their "soil sample."
4. Using toothpicks, toothbrushes, and other small tools, have the students clean their "find" and label it using an index card.
5. Finally, if your school permits it, allow students to eat their "soil."

Day 40–41

Thought for the Day

I think science has enjoyed an extraordinary success because it has such a limited and narrow realm in which to focus its efforts. Namely, the physical universe.
—Ken Jenkins

Cool Fact

The oldest fish fossils on record were found at Chengjiang in Yunnan Province, China. Two species have been found that date back more than 530 million years.

Activity

Glue Fossils

This activity demonstrates the formation of fossils and allows students to create and evaluate their own.

Materials:
- white glue
- a mixture of hard and soft objects for making impressions (cotton balls, coins, plants, leaves, keys, toys, shells, paper clips, etc.); one for each student
- modeling clay

Procedures:
1. Have your students create a recording sheet on notebook paper. At this point, they should include their name, date, and title of the activity.
2. Ask students to shape their clay into a pancake shape.
3. Have them choose an object, write its name on their recording sheet, and decide whether they would classify it as hard or soft.
4. Have students press the object into the clay. (Explain that in nature organisms are buried and may leave an imprint of their bodies in the sediment.)
5. Students should slowly pull the object out of the clay, being sure not to stretch or smear the clay. (In nature, things rot

and break down, leaving an impression behind—they are acting as the bacteria and removing the "body.")

6. Ask them to examine the shape left behind and record whether it is poor, good, or excellent. Have them base this decision on how well their shape was preserved. An excellent mold would show the entire shape, as well as details from the object; a good mold would show most of the shape and may have some detail; and a poor mold would be incomplete and show no detail.

7. Fill the mold with white glue. (The space animals leave beneath the soil when they rot can be filled with minerals and groundwater. The glue is representative of the minerals.)

8. Let the cast dry overnight.

9. When it is completely dry, students should peel back the glue from the clay.

10. On their recording sheet, have students note the quality of the cast—poor, good, or excellent. Have them base this decision on how well their shape was fossilized. An excellent cast would show the entire shape, as well as details from the object; a good cast would show most of the shape and may have some detail; and a poor cast would be incomplete and show no detail.

11. Discuss the difference in quality between hard and soft objects. The harder objects should have been more detailed and well-preserved than the soft objects.

Days 42–43

Thought for the Day

No one should approach the temple of science with the soul of a money changer.
—Thomas Browne

Cool Fact

Different minerals like manganese, iron, or copper can sometimes be found in water during the petrification of wood, and can turn wood a variety of different colors.

Activity

Petrified Celery
This activity will demonstrate how some fossils can be preserved by petrification or mineralization.

Materials (for teacher to use in demonstration):
- clear glass
- water to fill the glass about ⅓ full
- red or blue dye
- fresh celery with leaves (cut to the appropriate length to stand upright in the glass)
- ham bone or broken chicken bone (to show pores)

Procedures:
1. Show your students the pores in the ham or chicken bone, explaining that when something is fossilized due to petrification, minerals are absorbed into the pores, preserving the structure of the organism before it has a chance to rot.
2. Explain that the celery has vascular tubes that absorb water just like the pores of buried organisms absorb minerals.
3. Cut off the bottom of the celery so it is the right length to stand in the glass (keep the leaves on).
4. Fill the glass ⅓ full of water.
5. Place several drops of red or blue dye in the water, mixing it to give the water a rich, deep color.

6. Place the celery in the water, letting it sit overnight.

7. Have students observe the celery in the morning—it should have absorbed the color into its pores. This mimics the way minerals in groundwater fill porous organisms, hardening before the organic material can rot, preserving the pore structure of a plant or animal.

Day 44

Thought for the Day

If you're not part of the solution, you're part of the precipitate.
—Quinn J. Tillman

Cool Fact

Alaska has as many as 4,000 recorded earthquakes each year—more than the rest of the United States combined.

Teaser

When Jia got home from school, she announced to her parents that there had been an earthquake today that everyone at school had felt. "It was amazing!" she said. "There was this huge jolt and I almost fell off my feet." Her mom asked her if she knew how strong it was.

"The news said it was a 2.0," said Jia.

"Honey, we've talked about you making things up. People aren't going to believe anything you say anymore if you keep lying," her mother responded.

How did Jia's mom know she had made up the story?

Solution

A 2.0 earthquake is very weak and wouldn't have been felt, let alone jolt you off your feet. If Jia had known about a 2.0 earthquake, she would have had to find out after it occurred.

Day 45

Thought for the Day

Nature composes some of her loveliest poems for the microscope and the telescope.
—Theodore Roszak

Cool Fact

The tallest volcano on Hawaii is Mauna Kea, which climbs to more than 5.6 miles high.

Teaser

David returned from his trip to Hawaii and was telling his friends all about seeing a volcano erupt and witnessing a river of lava.

"It was amazing," he said, "I was standing only a few feet away as it flowed by."

"Nice try, David," said Josh. "There's no way that could have happened."

How did Josh know that David was lying?

Solution

The temperature of flowing lava is more than 700 degrees Celsius, which would have blistered and burned his skin if he was within a few feet. To safely view flowing lava, a person needs to be much further away.

Day 46

Thought for the Day

Science is the great antidote to the poison of enthusiasm and superstition.
—Adam Smith

Cool Fact

Kahoolawe, the smallest of the Hawaiian islands, is made up of a single shield volcano with a deep crater, called a caldera.

Teaser

David, feeling a little disappointed that Josh had sniffed out his exaggeration, said, "Well, the way the rock and ash flew all over the place was amazing!"

Josh looked closely at David and said, "I guess you didn't see a volcano erupt after all, did you?"

How did Josh know David was lying this time?

Solution

The type of volcano found on Hawaii is a shield volcano, which has flowing lava, but no ash spouting out. David was thinking about a different type of volcano, found elsewhere, called a composite volcano, which erupts lots of rock and ash, but little lava.

Day 47

Thought for the Day

Science is a cemetery of dead ideas.
—Miguel de Unamuno

Cool Fact

The discovery of the Mpemba Effect, the phenomenon that hot water may freeze more quickly than cold water, was made by a high school student named Erasto Mpemba in Tanzania, Africa, in 1969. He first took note of this strange effect while making ice cream. When he brought it up to his teachers, they did not believe him.

Teaser

Brian and Greg set up a mini-contest. The loser would do the winner's chores for a week. The contest was to determine who could get a glass of water to freeze the quickest. They wrote out the following rules to ensure fairness:

- They can only use water that comes out of the kitchen tap.
- They both must use identical containers, filled to the same spot.
- They must use the same freezer at the same time.

What should Brian do to have the best chance of beating Greg?

Solution

He should use hot water.

Day 48

Thought for the Day

Science is organized knowledge.
—Herbert Spencer

Cool Fact

The Coanda Effect is the tendency of a fluid or air to follow the curved surface of a wall. According to this theory, an airplane flies because its wings are forced upwards because they are tilted and deflect air downwards.

Activity

The Coanda Effect

This activity demonstrates one scientific theory, called the Coanda Effect, of how airplanes can fly.

Materials (for teacher to use in demonstration):
- cylindrical oatmeal container
- candle in a holder
- matches

Procedures:
1. Light the candle and place it in its holder on the table.
2. Place the oatmeal container on the table directly in front of the candle.
3. Have a student blow against the container on the opposite side of the candle, and at the same height as the flame.
4. Have your students discuss what happened and why they think this was the result. Because of the Coanda Effect, the air meets on the other side of the container at the height of the flame and blows out the candle.

Day 49

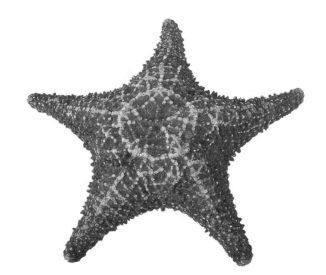

Thought for the Day

Science does not know its debt to imagination.
—Ralph Waldo Emerson

Cool Fact

The density of seawater is dependant on the témpérature and salinity of the water. When the temperature of seawater increases, its density decreases, however when the salinity of the water increases, the density increases as well.

Activity

Density of Liquids

This activity demonstrates the concepts of buoyancy and density, and relates them to one another.

Materials (for teacher to use in demonstration):
- syrup
- vegetable oil
- water
- small plastic toy
- cork
- grape
- glass container

Procedures:
1. Pour ⅓ cup of syrup into the container.
2. Pour ⅓ cup of vegetable oil on top of the syrup.
3. Pour ⅓ cup of water on top of the oil.
4. Let the liquids settle for several minutes.
5. Ask the students what they think will happen when you drop the objects into the container.
6. Drop the plastic toy, grape, and cork into the container and notice where each object settles. Have your students

compare the results with their predictions. What do they think happened?

7. The liquids each have a different density—the densest will settle at the bottom and the least dense will settle at the top. The objects will sink to the level of the liquid that has a greater degree of density than themselves, and they will float on that layer.

Day 50

Thought for the Day

The important thing in science is not so much to obtain new facts as to discover new ways of thinking about them.
—William Lawrence Bragg

Cool Fact

Carbonated water is created by adding carbon dioxide gas to water under pressure. The gas makes the water fizz and bubble.

Activity

Dancing Raisins

This activity demonstrates how carbon dioxide in carbonated water collects on the uneven surfaces of raisins, making them "dance" in the liquid.

Materials (for each group of students):
- glass jar
- raisins
- carbonated water

Procedures:
1. Divide your students into groups of three or four.
2. Have them fill the jar ¾ full of carbonated water.
3. Ask your students to make a prediction about what will happen when they put the raisins into the container.
4. Have them drop several raisins into the water.
5. Have your students wait a minute or two, and report what they observe. (The raisins should seem to dance around the water as the bubbles collect in the uneven surfaces on the raisins.)

Day 51

Thought for the Day

Every great advance in science has issued from a new audacity of imagination.
—John Dewey

Cool Fact

When two liquids separate themselves into layers—like oil and water—they are immiscible (will not mix together to form a one substance).

Activity

Like Oil and Water

This activity demonstrates the immiscible quality of certain liquids.

Materials (for each group of students):
- glass container
- dark food coloring
- vegetable oil
- water

Procedures:
1. Divide the students into groups of two to four.
2. Have each group fill their container half full of water and mix in a few drops of the food coloring.
3. Then, have them pour in some vegetable oil.
4. Finally, have them stir or shake the mixture in the container.
5. Ask for their observations. (The oil will seem to float in small little beads throughout the water, never mixing together.)

Day 52

Thought for the Day

Science has made us gods even before we are worthy of being men.
—Jean Rostand

Cool Fact

Ice sculptors use the process of reverse osmosis to remove all the impurities of the water to help produce ultra-clear ice blocks for sculpting.

Activity

Osmosis

This activity will demonstrate the effect of osmosis, when water moves from areas of low salt concentrations to high salt concentrations.

Materials (for teacher to use in demonstration):
• 2 potatoes
• 2 small bowls
• salt
• water

Procedures:
1. Fill both bowls with water.
2. Slice the potatoes into several flat pieces.
3. Add two tablespoons of salt to one of the bowls.
4. Put half of the potato slices into each bowl.
5. Let the potatoes soak for a half an hour.
6. After a half an hour, check out the potatoes. What is the difference between the two? Because you add salt to the one bowl, the water contains a higher salt concentration. The water from the potato will move to the water in the bowl, where the higher salt concentration is, leaving behind a mushy potato.

Day 53

Thought for the Day

The microwave oven is the consolation prize in our struggle to understand physics.
—Jason Love

Cool Fact

The first four-wheel drive vehicle was built by the Jacobus Spyker company in 1902.

Teaser

Cindy's rear-wheel-drive pick-up truck is stuck in the snow. She has a few concrete blocks loaded in the back but is not sure where should she place them for maximum weight and traction on the rear tires. Where should she place the blocks? In front of the axle as far forward as possible, directly over the rear axle, or behind the axle as far to the rear as possible?

Solution

Cindy should place the blocks as far to the rear as possible. This will have the effect of taking some weight off of the front axle. That weight has to go somewhere and the only other place it can go is onto the rear axle. If you had enough weight, or a long enough truck, you could even raise the front wheels off the ground.

Day 54

Thought for the Day

The most exciting phrase to hear in science, the one that heralds new discoveries, is not "Eureka!" but "That's funny. . ."
—Isaac Asimov

Cool Fact

The Earth is approximately 8,000 miles wide, and the Sun is roughly 900,000 miles across. This means it would take more than 100 Earths to span the width of the Sun. If the Sun were a hollow ball, you could fit about one million Earths inside of it!

Teaser

A light-year is the distance that light travels in a year. How many light-years are we away from the nearest star?

Solution

About 8 light-minutes (or $\frac{8}{526,000}$th of a light-year) from the nearest star is our own Sun. The second nearest star is about 4.2 light-years away or 25 trillion miles.

Day 55

Thought for the Day

I have had my results for a long time: but I do not yet know how I am to arrive at them.
—Karl Friedrich Gauss

Cool Fact

Cooking is the leading cause of home fires and fire-related injuries in the U.S. More often than not, cooking fires are a result of human errors or unattended pots and pans.

Teaser

What would happen if you tried to light a match in a sealed room, filled completely with methane gas?

Solution

Nothing. A flame needs oxygen to burn.

Day 56

Thought for the Day

Scientists should always state the opinions upon which their facts are based.
—Author Unknown

Cool Fact

Scientists are still debating the effects of cryogenics on metals, but some people believe that metal objects—like farm tools—seem to perform better when exposed to freezing temperatures.

Teaser

Joel told his friend Jim that he could make a metal ball go into a bottle without damaging the bottle at all. "Impossible!" Jim said. He held the ball to the opening of the bottle, and it was exactly the same size.

Joel took the bottle and set it on the table and placed the ball in the freezer. "Let's go play outside, and I'll do it later," Joel said. They went outside and played for several hours. When they came back inside, Joel took the ball out of the freezer and dropped it easily into the bottle.

How did he do that?

Solution

The metal ball contracted in the cold air inside the freezer, making it smaller, while the bottle opening stayed the same.

Day 57

Thought for the Day

Science is built up of facts, as a house is built of stones; but an accumulation of facts is no more a science than a heap of stones is a house.
—Henri Poincaré

Cool Fact

An electromagnet is a device in which magnetism is created by an electrical current.

Teaser

"I can make this rock levitate!" Nora shouted to her friends. She waved her two magic "wands" over the rock and the rock lifted slightly toward it. How did she do this?

Solution

The rock was iron and one of the "wands" was a metal rod. The other was made of copper, which formed an electromagnet.

Day 58

Thought for the Day

A science is any discipline in which the fool of this generation can go beyond the point reached by the genius of the last generation.
—Max Gluckman

Cool Fact

The human brain is composed of 70% water.

Teaser

Is it possible to cause a needle floating in a dish of water to sink without touching it, dropping anything on it, or shaking the dish?

Solution

Put some dish soap in the water. The molecules in the dish soap separate the water molecules, reducing the surface tension. Therefore, the needle sinks.

Day 59

Thought for the Day

There's no system foolproof enough to defeat a sufficiently great fool.
—Edward Teller

Cool Fact

Condensation can be brought about by cooling, or by an increased pressure. In nature, dew, fog, mist, and clouds are formed when water vapor condenses in the atmosphere.

Teaser

As you fight your way through the deep, hot jungle, you stumble across a running stream. All you have are two clean cups. How can you take a drink, even though you have no way to sterilize the jungle water?

Solution

Fill one cup with the stream water and hold it over the second cup, gently shaking the filled one. The condensation that forms on the outside of the filled cup will drop into the other cup. The condensation is safe to drink.

Day 60

Thought for the Day

Science commits suicide when it adopts a creed.
—Thomas Huxley

Cool Fact

Although airplanes were not originally designed to carry cargo, makers realized that this could be a valuable way to transport mail and other gear, and by the 1920s, manufacturers began planning and designing specialized cargo aircraft.

Teaser

A cargo plane loaded with birds for pet stores was ready to take off, but when the pilot calculated the weight of the plane and birds, he realized they had exceeded the weight allowance.

"No problem," said his copilot. "I'll just go back and make some noise. It will scare the birds into flight. Then you can take off. Once we've burned some of our fuel, we'll weigh less and the birds can rest again."

"Nice try," the pilot said, "but I'll just radio in for some of these birds to be unloaded."

How did he know the copilot's idea wouldn't work?

Solution

He knew that the birds were heavier than the air they displaced from the closed interior of the aircraft and that their combined weight while flying would still be distributed to the airplane by air molecules. Thus, whether they were flying or sitting still, they still weighed too much.

Day 61

Thought for the Day

The way to do research is to attack the facts at the point of greatest astonishment.
—Celia Green

Cool Fact

Gallium can be used to create a mirror by painting it on glass or porcelain.

Teaser

"It is so hot today, I bet it can melt this metal ball!" Eric exclaimed to Todd.

"No way," said Todd. "It's hot, but not hot enough to melt metal."

Eric put the ball on the picnic table and they went inside for something cool to drink. When they came out a while later, all that was left on the picnic table was a puddle of metallic goo. How did Eric know the ball would melt?

Solution

The ball was made of gallium, and its melting point is 85 degrees Fahrenheit. Because the temperature outside was near 100 degrees Fahrenheit, Eric knew it was only a matter of time before the ball would melt if it was left outside.

Day 62

Thought for the Day

Science is simply common sense at its best.
—Thomas Huxley

Cool Fact

Although a compass does point north, it doesn't point to the North Pole. When holding a compass in the Northern hemisphere, it actually points to the magnetic North Pole, located just off the Arctic Coast.

Activity

Make a Simple Compass—Part One

This activity demonstrates how compasses work.

Materials (for each group of students):
- magnet
- large sewing needle
- transparent bowl with water in it
- light thread such as cotton
- sheet of plain paper
- compass
- small square of very light cardboard

Procedures:
1. Divide the class into small groups.
2. Have each group tape the piece of paper to a desk.
3. Ask them to use their compass to mark a north-south line on the paper about an inch long, keeping the magnet well away from the compass while you do this.
4. Next, have them use the magnet to stroke the needle in one direction 20–30 times to magnetize it.
5. Have them put the magnet out of the way when they have finished with it.
6. Tell your students to suspend the needle on a length of thread but handle it carefully or it will lose its magnetism.

7. Have them hold the suspended needle over the piece of paper. The needle should align itself in a north-south position.

Day 63

Thought for the Day

Great scientific discoveries have been made by men seeking to verify quite erroneous theories about the nature of things.
—Aldous Huxley

Cool Fact

If you hold a compass in the Southern hemisphere, it will point to the magnetic South Pole, not the true South Pole. The magnetic South Pole is located in Antarctica.

Activity

Make a Simple Compass—Part Two

This activity demonstrates further how compasses work.

Materials (for each group of students):
- magnet
- large sewing needle
- transparent bowl with water in it
- light thread such as cotton
- sheet of plain paper
- compass
- small square of very light cardboard

Procedures:
1. Have your students form the same groups they worked in yesterday.
2. Have them repeat the process from yesterday, but instead of suspending the needle with thread this time, float it carefully on the square of cardboard on top of the bowl of water.
3. Tell your students to place the bowl on the paper over the north-south line they drew earlier. They should observe that the needle aligns itself in a north-south position.

Day 64

Thought for the Day

Physics is imagination in a straight jacket.
—John Moffat

Cool Fact

In 1777, Antoine Lavoisier, the French chemist called "the father of modern chemistry," proved that burning is a process that needs a substance to quickly interact with oxygen.

Activity

Extinguish the Flame

This activity demonstrates that fires cannot continue to burn without oxygen.

Materials (for teacher to use in demonstration):
- small bowl
- short candle
- large bowl
- baking soda
- vinegar

Procedures:
1. Fill the small bowl with baking soda and place the short candle upright in the baking soda.
2. Place the small bowl inside the big bowl.
3. Light the candle.
4. Pour enough vinegar to cover the baking soda in the small bowl.
5. As the vinegar and baking soda combine, the two react to form carbon dioxide gas. As the bowl fills with carbon dioxide, its level will become level with the flame, extinguishing the flame.

Day 65

Thought for the Day

Every science begins as philosophy and ends as art.
—Will Durant

Cool Fact

The wheel is one of the most important inventions. We don't know for sure who developed the first wheel, but the oldest wheel ever found was discovered by archaeologists in Mesopotamia and is more than 5,500 years old.

Teaser

Allan noticed a car that had wheels with spokes driving down the road. When he looked closer, he noticed the spokes on the top were going so fast they were blurred. But, when he looked at the bottom half of the wheel, the spokes appeared to be going so much slower he could have counted them. If all of the spokes were on the same wheel, how did this happen?

Solution

When viewed by a stationary object, the top spokes seem to be zipping by because they are going the speed of the car plus the rotation speed. The spokes on the bottom of the wheel are going the opposite direction as the car—moving the same speed, but in the opposite direction, thus appearing still.

Day 66

Thought for the Day

Science, in the very act of solving problems, creates more of them.
—Abraham Flexner

Cool Fact

Thomas Savery was an English military engineer and inventor who patented the first steam engine, a mechanism that converts potential energy into mechanical force, in 1698.

Teaser

You're on a train that's moving forward at 50 mph. You throw a ball in the direction that the train is moving. Relative to you and the train, the ball leaves your hand traveling at 20 mph. From the point of view of someone standing alongside the tracks, how fast is the ball moving?

Solution

Seventy miles per hour.

Day 67

Thought for the Day

Science is always wrong. It never solves a problem without creating ten more.
—George Bernard Shaw

Cool Fact

Frogs can hear using big round ears on the sides of their head called *tympanum*, which means drum. The size and distance between the ears depends on the wavelength and frequency of a male frog's call.

Teaser

How is it possible to conduct electricity while dissecting a frog?

Solution

When the acid in the frog mixes around the dissecting tools, electricity is conducted. This effect was first discovered in the late 1700s when biologist Luigi Galvani discovered that when he touched a nerve in a dissected frog's leg with a steel scalpel and a brass hook, the combination of metals mixing with the acids in the frog's body created a jolt of electricity, causing the nerves to jump. This was the early research that led to the discovery of batteries.

Day 68

Thought for the Day

Reason, Observation, and Experience—the Holy Trinity of Science.
—Robert G. Ingersoll

Cool Fact

The largest living bird is the ostrich. This popular bird stands an amazing 9 feet high and can weigh as much as 353 pounds.

Teaser

Is it possible for a bird to fly faster than a plane?

Solution

Yes, if the bird is flying inside the plane from the rear to the front.

Day 69

Thought for the Day

There is no national science just as there is no national multiplication table; what is national is no longer science.
—Anton Chekhov

Cool Fact

Of the 1,800 thunderstorms that are happening around the world at any given time, most last about 30 minutes and cover a diameter of 15 miles.

Teaser

How is it possible to tell how far away a thunderstorm is from where you stand, without the assistance of anything or anyone?

Solution

Light travels at 186,000 miles per second and sound travels about one mile every 5 seconds. Because thunder is the product of lightning, when you see the lightning you should begin to count until you hear the thunder. You then are able to tell how far the thunder has traveled. Example: If you see lightning and are able to count to 10 before you hear the thunder, you know that the storm is about 2 miles away.

Day 70

Thought for the Day

Science, at bottom, is really anti-intellectual. It always distrusts pure reason, and demands the production of objective fact.
—H. L. Mencken

Cool Fact

In the last part of the first century BC, the discovery that glass could be blown into various shapes was made. The art of glassblowing spread and was the standard way to shape glass until the late 19th century.

Teaser

If boiling water is poured into a very thick glass container and a very thin one, which is more likely to crack and why?

Solution

The thick glass is more likely to crack because glass is a poor conductor of heat. In a thin glass, the heat will pass rapidly from the glass into the surrounding air, causing the glass to expand. When hot water is poured into a thick glass, the inner surface expands, but the outer surface does not. This causes extreme stress on the glass, and it cracks.

Day 71

Thought for the Day

It is the man of science, eager to have his every opinion regenerated, his every idea rationalized, by drinking at the fountain of fact, and devoting all the energies of his life to the cult of truth, not as he understands it, but as he does not yet understand it, that ought properly to be called a philosopher.
—Charles Peirce

Cool Fact

Steel is an amazing, and reusable, resource. When steel cans are recycled, they become new cans, bicycle parts, and even cars.

Teaser

A ship maker built two ships of equal strength. One was made of wood, the other of steel. Which one was heavier?

Solution

The wooden ship is much heavier. Pound for pound, steel is exceptionally stronger than wood, therefore, it would take more wooden materials to match the steel boat's strength.

Day 72

Thought for the Day

The most remarkable discovery made by scientists is science itself.
—Gerard Piel

Cool Fact

Twisted rope is made by coiling three strands together in the same direction. Twisted rope is then fused and taped on each end so it won't unravel.

Teaser

Which situation would be most likely to cause a rope to break?
- 20 men of the same strength with 10 pulling on each end.
- 10 of the same men pulling on one end and the other end being fastened to a tree.

Solution

It makes no difference because the stress on the rope will be no greater. When an object is being pulled on by a rope, a force is exerted. The magnitude of this force is called *tension*. When 10 men of equal strength pull from opposite sides of the rope, the tension is the same because the force is the same. But, when 10 of those men pull the rope against the tree, the tension is the same because it is always the same at either end.

Day 73

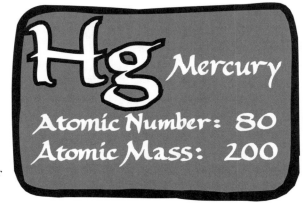

Hg Mercury
Atomic Number: 80
Atomic Mass: 200

Thought for the Day

An experiment is a question which science poses to Nature, and a measurement is the recording of Nature's answer.
—Max Planck

Cool Fact

It has been known for some time that high concentrations of mercury can be toxic to humans; the first record of a human being poisoned was in 50 BC.

Teaser

You have a box with the capacity of 125 cubic centimeters. Inside the box is a steel ball bearing that is 25 cubic centimeters in size. Next to the box is a 2-liter pail filled with mercury. How many cubic centimeters of mercury would you have to pour into the box to completely submerge the ball bearing?

Solution

You couldn't submerge the ball. Mercury is so dense, steel floats in it.

Day 74

Thought for the Day

If we wish to make a new world we have the material ready. The first one, too, was made out of chaos.
—Robert Quillen

Cool Fact

During the bat-ball collision, nearly two tons of force occur, forcing the ball to soar.

Teaser

What is easier and why? Balancing a baseball bat on your hand with the larger or the smaller end on the top?

Solution

It is easier to balance the bat with the larger end on top because of inertia. With your hand acting as a pivot, the bat rotates slower, making it easier to correct if it starts to fall.

Day 75

Thought for the Day

Science is a wonderful thing if one does not have to earn one's living at it.
—Albert Einstein

Cool Fact

Because our moon is bigger than Pluto, some scientists think it is more like a planet. They sometimes call the Earth-moon system a "double planet" because of the size of the moon.

Teaser

"Can you show me maria?" Kristen asked her friends Emma and Isabel. Isabel pointed to their friend across the courtyard, and Emma pointed to the picture of the moon in the magazine they had been looking at. Which girl was right?

Solution

They both were. Isabel pointed to a girl named Maria, while Emma was referring to the dark, flat regions on the moon's surface that are called maria.

Day 76

Thought for the Day

To know the history of science is to recognize the mortality of any claim to universal truth.
—Evelyn Fox Keller

Cool Fact

The average hen lays 257 eggs a year, more than double the average from the late 1800s, when hens laid an average of 100 eggs a year.

Teaser

Samantha had a dish of rotten eggs that she planned to throw at her brother the next time he made her mad. She set them on the counter in the kitchen and left for a few minutes to get a box to keep them in. When she came back, she was upset to see that her brother—knowing what she had been up to—had mixed her nice, rotten eggs with the fresh eggs in the refrigerator. They all looked and smelled the same to her. She'd never figure it out.

Her brother popped back into the kitchen, laughing. "I'll show you how to tell rotten eggs from the fresh eggs without breaking any—if you promise not to use them on me and give me $1.00," he said.

She had no choice; her mom would ground her if she found out about her plan. She agreed and her brother showed her quickly how to do it—and he was right, too! How did her brother do it?

Solution

He simply put the eggs in a bowl of water. Fresh eggs sink, while rotten eggs float. As an egg rots, it makes hydrogen sulfide, a gas that gets trapped inside the egg, causing it to float in water.

Day 77

Thought for the Day

The greatest discoveries of science have always been those that forced us to rethink our beliefs about the universe and our place in it.
—Robert L. Park

Cool Fact

Many female insects have the important job of laying and protecting their eggs. Some can lay an amazing amount of eggs; a queen African termite can lay up to 30,000 eggs a day!

Teaser

Simon had collected some termites, which he placed in a ventilated jar with leaves containing all of the elements termites need to survive. Unfortunately, the termites began to die after only a few days. Why?

Solution

Termites eat their food secondhand. They collect leaves and pile them up underground, allowing fungi to grow and digest the cellulose from the plants. Then, the termites eat pieces of the fungi, digesting the cellulose secondhand. There was no soil in the jar, so no fungi were able to grow, and therefore the termites died.

Day 78

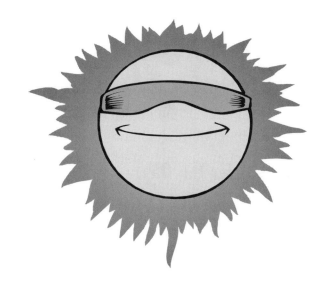

Thought for the Day

The great men of science are supreme artists.
—Martin H. Fischer

Cool Fact

While the sun has been full of life for the last 4.6 billion years, it has enough life left for another 5 billion. When it "dies," it will swell and eventually engulf the Earth.

Teaser

A small weight hangs suspended by a string in a sealed bottle. How can you get it to fall to the bottom of the bottle without touching the string, weight, or bottle?

Solution

Use a magnifying glass to direct the sun's rays and burn the string. The weight will fall when the string breaks.

Day 79

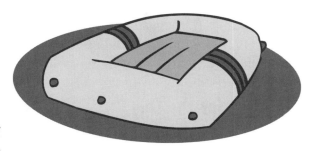

Thought for the Day

It is characteristic of science that the full explanations are often seized in their essence by the percipient scientist long in advance of any possible proof.
—John Desmond Bernal

Cool Fact

Samples of water are obtained from the deep ocean using special samplers or bottles attached to a wire lowered from a ship. Most types of bottles must be sent down open, as the water pressure would crush a closed bottle. The bottles are closed at a selected depth either by a mechanism triggered by a weight slid down the supporting wire or by an electrical signal from the surface.

Teaser

Neil kept telling Nathan not to row out on the lake in the inflatable boat. "You're going to sink," he said.

"No, I'm not. I patched each one of those holes with the patch kit that the man at the marina sold me. I followed the directions on the adhesive exactly."

"Go ahead, but I'll have a towel waiting for you!" Neil shouted as Nathan began paddling out. A few minutes later, Nathan was frantically paddling back in toward shore as the boat filled with water.

How had Neil known that Nathan's patch job was doomed to failure?

Solution

Nathan had patched the inside of the boat. He should have patched the holes on the outside of the boat so the water pressure could help hold the patches in place. Instead, the pressure pushed toward the inside of the boat, forcing the patches off the holes, causing the boat to sink.

Day 80

Thought for the Day

Science is the topography of ignorance.
—Oliver Wendell Holmes, Sr.

Cool Fact

J. J. Thomson discovered that the electron was a subatomic particle in 1897. He was working at Cambridge University.

Activity

Bright Idea

This activity demonstrates the power of transferring electrons.

Materials (for teacher to use in demonstration):
- comb
- light bulb

Procedures:
1. Turn off the lights and draw the shades.
2. Take the comb and run it quickly through your (or a student's) hair.
3. Hold the comb to the metal end of the light bulb while watching the filament in the bulb carefully.
4. The friction between the hair and the comb cause electrons to travel and cling to the comb. The hair becomes positively charged while the comb becomes negatively charged, causing the bulb to emit small pulses of light when the comb touches the bulb.

Day81

Thought for the Day

In science it often happens that scientists say, "You know that's a really good argument; my position is mistaken," and then they actually change their minds and you never hear that old view from them again. They really do it. It doesn't happen as often as it should, because scientists are human and change is sometimes painful. But it happens every day. I cannot recall the last time something like that happened in politics or religion.
—Carl Sagan

Cool Fact

Today, people are continually trying to find new ways to use solar energy as a way to conserve the Earth's resources. This effort started in the 1830s when British astronomer John Herschel used his solar collector box for cooking food.

Activity

Radiation and the Transfer of Energy

This activity will give your students an understanding that dark objects absorb energy faster than light objects.

Materials (for teacher to use in demonstration):
- five small cups
- light colored sand
- dark colored sand
- heat lamp
- five thermometers
- water

Procedures:
1. Use the five cups and put the following in them:
    - light *dry* sand in one,
    - light *wet* sand in another,
    - dark *dry* sand in another,
    - dark *wet* sand in another, and
    - water in the last.

2. Arrange the cups in as small of a circle as possible without having them touch each other.
3. Place a thermometer in each cup so the bulb is below the surface of the material.
4. Place a lamp above the containers and directly over the center of the circle.
5. Read and record the temperature of each material just before turning on the lamp. Turn on the lamp and record the temperature at regular intervals of one minute for 5 minutes.
6. Then turn off the lamp and continue to record the temperature at regular intervals of one minute for 5 more minutes.
7. Discuss the differences in temperature. The dark sands (both wet and dry) should have absorbed more heat, making their temperature warmer than the others. Both wet sands, however, should have stayed their temperature for longer periods of time once the lamp was turned off. The dry sand will lose its heat faster.

Day 82

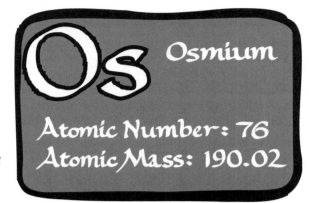

Os Osmium

Atomic Number: 76
Atomic Mass: 190.02

Thought for the Day

Physics isn't a religion. If it were, we'd have a much easier time raising money.
—Leon Lederman

Cool Fact

The element osmium doesn't react with air, instead it forms a poisonous compound called osmium tetroxide. The name *osmium*, comes from the Greek word *osme*, which means "a smell."

Teaser

What do these names have in common?

Ben
Al
Oscar

Solution

They can all be spelled using atomic symbols:

Ben	BeN	(Beryllium: Be; Nitrogen: N)
Al	Al	(Aluminum: Al)
Oscar	OsCAr	(Osmium: Os; Carbon: C; Argon: Ar)

Day 83

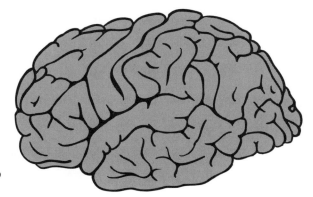

Thought for the Day

Theory guides. Experiment decides.
—An old saying in science, seen attributed to many different persons.

Cool Fact

Without blood flowing to the brain, a human being will become unconscious within 8-10 seconds.

Teaser

What is being represented by this equation? (Hint: Think carefully.)

4 = L of the B (O, P, T, and F)

Solution

4 = Lobes of the Brain (Occipital, Parietal, Temporal, and Frontal)

Day 84

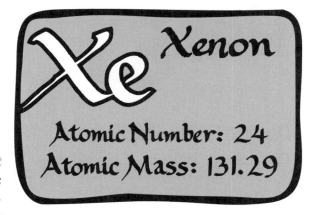

Thought for the Day

Every honest researcher I know admits he's just a professional amateur. He's doing whatever he's doing for the first time. That makes him an amateur. He has sense enough to know that he's going to have a lot of trouble, so that makes him a professional.

—Charles Franklin Kettering

Cool Fact

Xenon's name comes from the Greek word *xenon*, meaning "stranger." Its main use is in fluorescent lamps, photography flash equipment, and strobe lights.

Teaser

What element do these words make?
Xenon
Nitrogen
Oxygen
Nitrogen

Solution

Xenon

Xenon (Xe), Nitrogen (N), Oxygen (O), and Nitrogen (N)

Day 85

Thought for the Day

You cannot teach a man anything; you can only help him find it within himself.
—Galileo Galilei

Cool Fact

Although Florida oranges are greener than California oranges, they are still ripe and sweet. Because the temperatures in Florida evenings are warmer than nights in California, more chlorophyll is able to travel to the peel, leaving behind the greenish color.

Activity

When Is an Orange Not an Orange?

This activity facilitates your students' evaluation and observational skills.

Materials (for teacher to use in demonstration):
- an orange
- a wooden orange
- a plastic orange
- a picture of an orange
- a card with the word orange on it
- paper
- pencils

Procedures:
1. Hold up an orange in front of the class. Ask your students to list all of their observations and thoughts about the orange (e.g., color, texture, shape, etc.). Accept all answers.
2. Have students close their eyes. When they open their eyes, hold up a wooden orange. Have them cross off everything on their list that does *not* apply to the new orange.
3. Have students close their eyes again. When they open their eyes, hold up a plastic orange. Repeat.

4. Have students close their eyes again. When they open their eyes, hold up a picture of an orange. Repeat.

5. Have students close their eyes again. When they open their eyes, hold up a piece of paper with the word *orange* written on it. Repeat.

6. Ask your students:
   - At what point does the orange *stop* being an orange? Defend your answer.
   - Which item of the ones that were held up was *not* an orange at all? Discuss why or why not.
   - What does an orange mean to you? Be very specific and defend your answer.
   - Why is it important to be specific when describing something to another person or recording information?

Day 86

Thought for the Day

Nature's laws govern which things can be done, and which can't. The trouble is, when we set out to do something, we don't always know which of these categories it's in.
—Donald Simanek

Cool Fact

Arsenic contamination of well water may be caused by dissolved minerals from local bedrock or sediments being absorbed into groundwater, or it could be from the use of pesticides.

Teaser

You have a 100-foot deep well, and your water pump is damaged and in need of repair. You hire two plumbers to quote you a price on a new pump. One says that he will replace the existing submersible pump with a similar model for $200. The other says that he will sell you a high-efficiency vacuum pump, which will cost you $50 less and will have the added benefit that you can keep it in your basement for easy maintenance instead of having to put it back down the well. Which pump should you buy?

Solution

You should buy the $200 submersible pump. A vacuum pump can only draw water from a height of about 30 feet, no matter how powerful the pump is. With a 100-foot deep well, the pump would not provide any water to the house. The second plumber obviously has no idea what he's talking about.

Day87

Thought for the Day

The scientist does not study nature because it is useful; he studies it because he delights in it, and he delights in it because it is beautiful. If nature were not beautiful, it would not be worth knowing, and if nature were not worth knowing, life would not be worth living.
—Jules Henri Poincaré

Cool Fact

Your inner ear helps you to balance, so when you have an inner-ear infection, you can sometimes feel dizzy and fall down.

Teaser

Why do tightrope walkers use a long pole to help them stay balanced? How does this work?

Solution

A tightrope walker is able to stand by keeping his center of mass directly above the rope. If his center of mass moves off center, he needs to correct this or he will rotate off of the rope and fall down. By carrying a long pole, he is able to increase his rotational inertia. So, he is able to rotate slower and have more time to fix his center of mass. The balancing poles are usually droopy and weighted at the tips. This lowers the center of mass of the walker, making it easier to balance.

Day 88

Thought for the Day

The saddest aspect of life right now is that science gathers knowledge faster than society gathers wisdom.
—Isaac Asimov

Cool Fact

Although soil erosion is natural, it can become a problem if humans aren't careful. Their actions can force it to occur at a much more rapid rate.

Activity

Erosion Demonstration

This activity demonstrates the process of erosion on hills or other slopes.

Materials (for teacher to use in demonstration):
- two large disposable aluminum pans (lasagna size works well), one with several small holes at one end
- a measuring cup, beaker, or watering can
- dirt from your backyard, the school grounds, or someplace similar (purchased potting soil will not work well)
- two or three dictionaries or other large books

Procedures:
1. Pour the dirt in the bottom of the pan with the holes poked in it. Pack and smooth it until it is flat and 2 or 3 inches deep.
2. Prop the dirt-filled pan up on one end by placing the books under the edge of the side opposite of the holes. Place the empty pan under the dirt-filled pan where the holes are poked (this will catch the water run-off.)
3. Ask your students, "How does rain help shape the Earth?" "What is its impact?"
4. Have them make predictions about what will happen if "rain" falls on the dirt-filled pan.

5. Gently pour water on the higher end, and ask your students to observe what is happening to the dirt where the water hits and what happens to the water that is filling the lower pan. Much of the dirt will be washed away and some will filter through to the lower pan.

6. Ask, "Would it make a difference if the dirt started off wet as opposed to the dry dirt we just used?" "What would happen if the slope was steeper?"

Day 89

Thought for the Day

Darwin has interested us in the history of nature's technology.
—Karl Marx

Cool Fact

The Food and Agriculture Organization of the United Nations estimates that the global loss of productive land through erosion is 5–7 million acres a year.

Activity

Erosion on the Plains

This activity demonstrates the process of erosion on the plains.

Materials (for teacher to use in demonstration):
- aluminum pie pans
- paper cups
- toothpicks
- moist sand
- water

Procedures:
1. Pack the pie pan with sand so it is flat.
2. Use a toothpick to poke holes in the bottom of one of the cups.
3. Have one student hold the cup with the holes above the "plain," while another student pours water from the other cup into the one with holes so that it "rains" onto the plain.
4. Ask your students to make observations and discuss the effects of the rain on the plain. The rain will wear away gullies, ditches, or craters in the plains.
5. Ask them to make a prediction about what would be different if there was vegetation (like grass) present on the plain. (Less of the soil would be washed away because the vegetation will help anchor it.)

Day 90

Thought for the Day

Observations always involve theory.
—Edwin Hubble

Cool Fact

Because of deforestation, overgrazing, plowing, and fire, soil is much more susceptible to erosion from wind and water.

Activity

Erosion on a Mountain

This activity demonstrates the process of erosion on a mountain.

Materials (for teacher to use in demonstration):
- aluminum pie pans
- paper cups
- toothpicks
- moist sand
- water
- tissue paper

Procedures:
1. Make a "mountain" in the center of one of the pie pans. Pack the sand tightly.
2. Use a toothpick to poke holes in the bottom of one of the cups.
3. Have one student hold the cup with the holes above the center of the "mountain," while another student pours water from the other cup into the one with holes so that it "rains" onto the mountain.
4. Ask your students to make observations and discuss the effects of the rain on the mountain. (The mountain should have eroded; sand was washed away and collected at the bottom of the pie pan.) Ask them to make a prediction

about what would be different if there was vegetation (like grass) present on the mountain.

5. Have them try the experiment again, making a new mountain, this time covering the sides of it with tissue paper to represent vegetation. (This time, less sand should have been washed from the mountainside. The vegetation held more of it in place, and some that washed down from the top will have collected near the vegetation so it doesn't reach the pie pan.)

6. What is the difference between how a mountain erodes if it has or doesn't have growth?

Day91

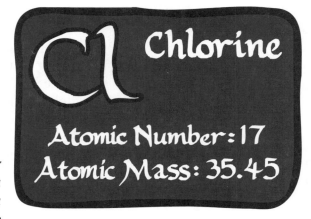

Thought for the Day

My mother made me a scientist without ever intending to. Every other Jewish mother in Brooklyn would ask her child after school, "So? Did you learn anything today?" But not my mother. "Izzy," she would say, "did you ask a good question today?" That difference—asking good questions—made me become a scientist.
—Isidor Isaac Rabi

Cool Fact

Chlorine is one of the most commonly used chemicals in the United States, because it is used in such things as bleach, paper, cloth, pesticides, rubber, and many solvents.

Teaser

There are two jars: One is filled with the poisonous gas of chlorine, and the other is filled with the dangerously reactive element called sodium. A fellow scientist tells you that he will pay you $5 million if you can figure out a way to swallow the contents both jars. How do you do it without killing yourself?

Solution

Pour the contents of both jars together in a heated chamber, heat the chamber to 5,000 degrees Fahrenheit, and the two elements combine to give you sodium chloride, otherwise known as table salt.

Day 92

Thought for the Day

Not fact-finding, but attainment to philosophy is the aim of science.
—Martin H. Fischer

Cool Fact

Although steel can only be stretched about 8% before it breaks, the thread woven by the orb spider can stretch more than 30% before it breaks.

Teaser

You are given a thread that is one foot in length. You are asked to hold the thread from two different ends and pull the thread with exactly equal amount of force applied from both ends and in exactly the opposite direction. At which point will the thread break?

Solution

Its weakest point.

Day 93

Thought for the Day

The best scientist is open to experience and begins with romance—the idea that anything is possible.
—Ray Bradbury

Cool Fact

The only reason dust "floats" on Earth is because it is light and able to move around by the air—but it won't float in a vacuum. Like any other object, without moving air to push it around, it will simply fall back to the ground.

Teaser

A scientist designs a type of vacuum cleaner that can be used to suck up and collect moon dust. He is immediately fired for his incompetence. What was wrong with his plan?

Solution

Because the moon has no atmosphere, it is already under vacuum. The reason a vacuum cleaner works is that the pressure drop between the air in the room and the vacuum bag causes air to rush into the bag, carrying some dirt with it. Because there is no pressure drop between the vacuum chamber and the moon's surface, you could not suck up moon dust.

Day 94

Thought for the Day

The saddest aspect of life right now is that science gathers knowledge faster than society gathers wisdom.
—Isaac Asimov

Cool Fact

The shortest path between any two objects is called a geodesic—a line that is curved because of the curvature of space.

Teaser

A scientist decided to try an experiment to determine the speed of light. He would have his assistant stand at one end of a beach with a powerful flashlight, and the scientist would stand at the other end of the beach, 500 yards away, with a stopwatch. The assistant would raise his hand and turn on the light at the same time. The scientist would time the difference between when he saw the assistant's hand go up and when he saw the light, and would calculate the speed of light, knowing the distance between them.

Now, we all know that light travels too quickly for the scientist to have even noticed a difference. However, if light traveled very slowly, the experiment still would have failed. Why?

Solution

The only reason that the scientist could see the assistant's hand is that light from the sun reflected off the hand and traveled to the scientist's eye. If light traveled slowly, the scientist would still see the hand go up at the same time as the light was turned on. He would just see them happen a few seconds after they actually happened.

Day 95

Thought for the Day

In every department of physical science there is only so much science, properly so-called, as there is mathematics.
—Immanuel Kant

Cool Fact

Many petroleum companies are experimenting with the use of renewable resources to produce gasoline alternatives. Corn is one of these resources, and can be used to produce ethanol. Just one acre of this crop (which can be replanted each year) can make enough fuel to run a car for more than 72,000 miles.

Teaser

In a high school science class, Jimmy was given 50 milliliters of water and 50 milliliters of ethanol. His task was to mix them together and then run an experiment on the mixture. When he mixed them, however, his mixture only contained 94 milliliters. Jimmy swears that he didn't lose any of the liquids by any means. What happened to the other 6 milliliters?

Solution

When liquids are mixed, the molecules can arrange themselves so that they fit together more tightly than either of the original, pure liquids. A good way to visualize this is to picture a box completely filled with billiard balls (representing large molecules). If you pour a small amount of sand (representing small molecules) into the box, the sand will fill the voids between the billiard balls. The mass in the box will increase, but the total volume will not change. This is how Jimmy could prove his innocence—if he weighs the mixture, it will equal the original weight of the water plus the weight of the ethanol.

Day 96

Thought for the Day

A new scientific truth does not triumph by convincing opponents and making them see the light, but rather because its opponents eventually die, and a new generation grows up that is familiar with it.
—Max Planck

Cool Fact

Because aerodynamics plays such an important role in the speed and function of Formula One racing cars, designers have worked hard over the years to minimize drag and improve the down force in order to better keep the tires on the track.

Teaser

How could you drive a car upside down?

Solution

A Formula One car, if going fast enough, can produce enough down force to keep itself in contact with the roof of a tunnel. The down force counteracts the force of gravity on the car. Some other sports cars also have this potential. Down force increases with speed, so the faster it goes, the more likely it is that this force would be strong enough to keep the car from falling.

Day 97

Thought for the Day

The scientist, by the very nature of his commitment, creates more and more questions, never fewer. Indeed the measure of our intellectual maturity, one philosopher suggests, is our capacity to feel less and less satisfied with our answers to better problems.
—G. W. Allport

Cool Fact

Higher quality rubber balloons are made from a naturally occurring substance called *latex*. Latex is a milky sap that comes from rubber trees that grow in many of the world's rain forests.

Teaser

"Can you put this pin into this balloon without popping it?" asked Chris.

"Sure," said Jane, and poked the pin straight into the balloon. How did she do it?

Solution

Before she put the pin into the balloon, she put a piece of masking tape on the surface of the balloon. She placed the pin through the tape into the balloon. Because the tape sticks to the rubber, it does not let the molecules stretch to the breaking point. The tape acts as a reinforcer.

Day98

Thought for the Day

The improver of natural science absolutely refuses to acknowledge authority, as such. For him, skepticism is the highest of duties: blind faith the one unpardonable sin.
—Thomas Huxley

Cool Fact

Although mercury is a metal, it stays in its liquid form at room temperature, making it perfect for the inside of thermometers, as it won't solidify readily.

Teaser

There is a box with a highly explosive bomb inside it. The lid of the box is made of glass and attached to this lid is a bowl of mercury with a dozen exposed wire leads just out of reach of the mercury. You know that any attempt to remove the lid or cut through it would move the mercury enough to trip the bomb. How do you safely disarm this booby trap to disengage the bomb?

Solution

By heating the steel box and raising the temperature inside, the mercury, which has a relatively low evaporation point, will disappear, making it safe to lift the lid. Just be careful not to inhale any of the fumes!

Day 99

Thought for the Day

Our sun is one of 100 billion stars in our galaxy. Our galaxy is one of billions of galaxies populating the universe. It would be the height of presumption to think that we are the only living things in that enormous immensity.
—Wernher von Braun

Cool Fact

Originally, sheet glass was created by pouring liquid-hot glass onto a flat surface and rolling it smooth. Now it is made by rolling it through double rollers many times.

Teaser

You are trapped in a glass sphere with nothing but a pocketknife. You will be allowed to go free if you can make something move at a rate of speed faster than 3,000 miles per hour. What should you do?

Solution

Make a crack in the glass. A crack in glass spreads at a rate faster than 3,000 miles per hour.

Day 100

Thought for the Day

Science is organized knowledge.
—Herbert Spencer

Cool Fact

In 1967, Sony introduced the first portable video camera, the Sony DV-2400 Video Rover. It was a two-piece set, made up of a large black and white camera and a separate record-only VCR unit. It then required the user to have a separate VTR (video tape recorder) to play the finished video. It was clunky, heavy, and awkward, but one person could handle carrying it.

Teaser

You have hooked up a video camera so that whatever it is pointed at shows up on your TV. What will you see if you point the camera at the TV?

Solution

You will see whatever was on the TV before you aimed the camera at it, surrounded by an image of the TV's border. The image, surrounded by the TV border, will continue to repeat, one inside the other.

Day 101

Thought for the Day

Science is the systematic classification of experience.
—George Quinn Lewes

Cool Fact

Justus von Liebig discovered the chemical process of coating a glass surface with metallic silver in 1835, beginning the modern techniques of mirror making. Before that, mirrors were contoured pieces of metal, highly polished and shined.

Teaser

What is solid and not translucent, that you can touch with your finger, but you can't see in broad daylight, even through a mirror?

Solution

A mirror's surface; you don't see it but rather "see" the things reflected by it.

Day 102

Thought for the Day

Science is nothing but trained and organized common sense differing from the latter only as a veteran may differ from a raw recruit: and its methods differ from those of common sense only as far as the guardsman's cut and thrust differ from the manner in which a savage wields his club.
—Thomas Quinn Huxley

Cool Fact

Although most people brew their coffee using a drip or filtered method, the percolator, which was invented in France in 1827, is still sometimes used today. It boils the coffee and produces a bitter-tasting brew.

Teaser

You are served a hot cup of coffee and room-temperature cream at a restaurant. You want to wait a few minutes before you drink the coffee, and you want it to be as hot as possible when you drink it. Should you pour the cream in the coffee:
a. Immediately
b. Just before you drink it
c. It doesn't matter

Solution

The driving force for heat transfer is temperature difference. The coffee by itself is very hot and will therefore cool down at a fast rate. Once the cream is added, the temperature will drop even more. If the cream is added immediately, then the temperature will drop initially but will then continue to drop at a slower rate because the coffee with cream is cooler than the coffee alone; therefore, the driving force for heat transfer is less. As an added bonus, adding the cream will increase the mass of the contents of the cup. A larger mass takes longer to cool down than a smaller one at the same temperature. The cream should be added immediately.

Day 103

Thought for the Day

Science is nothing but developed perception, interpreted intent, common sense rounded out and minutely articulated.
—George Santayana

Cool Fact

The interior structure of the moon is difficult to study. Its top layer, which is almost 500 miles thick, is made up of a rocky solid. The mid-layer is partly molten, and although scientists don't know for sure, they believe that there may be a small core of iron despite the lack of magnetic field.

Teaser

From the Earth we can see the moon rise and set. When the day comes that we can live on the moon, will we see the Earth rise and set?

Solution

No. The moon's rotation is synchronized with its orbit around the Earth, which is why we can only see one side of the moon from Earth. From an observer on the moon, the Earth would appear to be in the same place at all times.

Day 104

Thought for the Day

An expert is a man who has made all the mistakes which can be made in a very narrow field.
—Niels Bohr

Cool Fact

It takes more than 12 pounds of whole milk to make a gallon of ice cream. With the average American eating more than 48 pints of ice cream a year, that's a lot of milk!

Teaser

Many people use this every day. If we had 50 pounds of it, it would contain about 43 pounds of water; 2 pounds of fat; 2 pounds of casein, ash, and albumin; and 2 ½ pounds of sugar. What is it?

Solution

Milk.

Day 105

Thought for the Day

The capacity to blunder slightly is the real marvel of DNA. Without this special attribute, we would still be anaerobic bacteria and there would be no music.
—Lewis Thomas

Cool Fact

In 1936, the first electric blanket was invented. It had an automatic thermostat control that turned on and off based on the temperature of the room.

Teaser

Which would keep you warmer: two 1-inch thick blankets or one 2-inch thick blanket?

Solution

Two blankets would keep you warmer because the air caught between the two blankets acts as an additional insulator.

Day 106

Thought for the Day

The great men of science are supreme artists.
—Martin H. Fischer

Cool Fact

The saying "heat rises" is an acknowledgement of the fact that warmer air has a lower density than the surrounding atmosphere, and because of this lower density, it will rise. Thus, because cold air has a higher density, it will sink.

Teaser

"Close that front door!" shouted Sheila's mom from upstairs. "You're making it cold up here."

"I'll close the door, Mom, but that can't be what's making it cold upstairs." Sheila shouted back.

Sheila was right, but why?

Solution

Hot air rises and cold air descends, so the cold air from the open door wouldn't make the upstairs any colder. (It might make the downstairs colder, though!)

Day 107

Thought for the Day

The scientist is not a person who gives the right answers, he's one who asks the right questions.
—Claude Lévi-Strauss

Cool Fact

The familiar juice box is an aseptic container, which means that it is created and filled under sterile conditions. It does not need refrigeration or preservatives to stay contaminate-free.

Teaser

Aretha's jaw hurt horribly when she tried to suck through a straw. She was really thirsty, but did not have a glass and couldn't figure out how to get the juice out of the juice box without tipping it over. What could she do?

Solution

She should blow into the straw, pressurizing the box. When she stops blowing, the pressure will force the juice out through the straw and into her mouth. She could continue this until the juice box is empty.

Day 108

Thought for the Day

It requires a very unusual mind to undertake the analysis of the obvious.
—Alfred North Whitehead

Cool Fact

A sphere has very small surface area compared to other shapes, so bubbles, water droplets, and other natural occurrences that need to stay small are usually found in this form.

Teaser

There are two glass spheres on the table in front of you. They look the same, feel the same, and have the same weight. One is hollow and contains the map to a treasure chest. If you can determine which sphere is hollow without breaking either, you will be given the map. How do you do it?

Solution

Roll the spheres on a level flat surface. The hollow sphere will roll further because its mass is distributed away from the center, giving it a higher moment of inertia. Alternatively, you could spin them and see which is harder to stop. (The hollow sphere will be harder to stop for the same reason mentioned above.)

Day 109

Thought for the Day

[Science is] the labor and handicraft of the mind.
—Francis Bacon

Cool Fact

The loud bang you hear when a balloon is popped is not due to pressure. Rather, it is because the tightly stretched ends of the torn latex snap back to their original size faster than the speed of sound.

Teaser

You have two balloons—one filled more than the other. If you connected a tube between them, which way would the air flow: toward the more or the less full balloon?

Solution

Toward the larger one. The smaller balloon has greater elastic force, and will exert a greater inward force. It has greater internal pressure, which is why it is initially more difficult to inflate a balloon than after it has already started expanding.

Day 110

Thought for the Day

[Science is] the literature of truth.
—Josh Billings

Cool Fact

When you're in water, your lungs that are filled with air become like a balloon inside your body, keeping your chest afloat. Your legs, however, usually sink no matter how well you can float.

Teaser

Whenever you plop a cork into a glass of water, it drifts to the side of the glass. How can you get it to float directly in the middle using only water, the glass, and the cork?

Solution

The reason that a cork drifts to the side of a glass is that it floats to the highest point. Because water "clings" to the glass, the highest point is around the edge of the water. To get the cork to float in the middle of the glass, all you have to do is fill the glass as much as possible. The water will form a convex shape above the glass, with the highest point at its center. This is where the cork will settle.

Day 111

Thought for the Day

Shall I refuse my dinner because I do not fully understand the process of digestion?
—Oliver Heaviside

Cool Fact

Using only a bubble wand, dish soap, glycerine, and water, Alan McKay made a 105-foot bubble on August 9, 1996, in New Zealand.

Teaser

Which will rise to the surface of a glass of water more quickly: a bubble with a diameter of 1.5 millimeters or one with a diameter of 6 millimeters?

Solution

The smaller one; very small bubbles rise to the surface in a straight line, but larger bubbles tend to zigzag and spiral because they have a greater surface area for the water to catch on and disrupt their ascent.

Day 112

Thought for the Day

Facts are not science—as the dictionary is not literature.
—Martin H. Fischer

Cool Fact

Soil is rich with various life forms. In just one tablespoon of this resource, there are more living organisms than there are people on Earth!

Activity

Recognizing Soil Texture

This activity helps students understand the importance of soil texture in agriculture.

Materials (for each student or station):
* samples of silt, sand, and clay
* eyedroppers
* water

Procedures:
1. Either set up stations with small samples of each type of soil, or give each student a small sample.
2. Ask students to rub a small amount of each sample between their thumb and forefinger. Have them describe the samples. Which is the smoothest? Roughest?
3. Have them place a small of amount one sample in the palm of their hand and add two drops of water to it.
4. Tell them to use a finger from their other hand to mix the water and soil. How does the mixture feel? Repeat this for each sample.
5. Discuss their findings. How do they think these different samples would affect what could grow in a given area?

Days 113–116

Thought for the Day

Reality is merely an illusion, albeit a very persistent one.
—Albert Einstein

Cool Fact

Some bacteria spend their entire lives in the air, growing and breeding in clouds above our heads. They are so small we can't see them as they get blown around through the atmosphere.

Activity

Bacteria Is All Around Us

This activity will help your students learn about the conditions that foster bacteria growth.

Materials (for each group of students):
- one petri dish with agar
- a sterile cotton swab
- permanent marker
- index cards with a sample location written on it
- an incubator or other warm place (school boiler rooms work well)

Procedures:
1. Prepare the petri dishes ahead of time and leave one open on your desk.
2. Prepare the index cards. Write sample locations where students are most likely to find bacteria growing (e.g., toilet handles, drinking fountains, door knobs, phones, nurse's office, locker room, banisters).
3. Explain to students the importance of keeping the agar and cotton swab sterile. When they open the petri dishes, they should swab them quickly and close the dish right back up again.

4. Have each group choose two index cards with sample locations, and then turn their petri dish over, draw a line down the middle, and label each half according to their locations.

5. Send the groups out a couple at a time to gather their samples with their swabs. When they come back, have them swab their agar and seal their petri dishes with tape.

6. Have each group draw exactly what they see, and then cover and put the petri dishes in their warm location. Model this by covering the petri dish that has been open on your desk. This will be placed in a warm spot, as well.

7. Have your students check out their petri dishes, as well as the one from your desk, for a few minutes each day over Days 2 and 3, drawing what they see. You could model this by drawing what you see in your dish.

8. On Day 4, have each group analyze their findings. They should draw what they see and answer the following questions:

   • How many clusters of bacteria are growing in each petri dish?
   • Which of the locations produced the highest number of colonies? The least?
   • What was the importance of using sterile agar and cotton swabs?
   • What kind of environmental conditions seem to affect bacteria growth?
   • How can you control the amount of bacteria that you will encounter?
   • What was the result of the petri dish that had been left open on the teacher's desk?
   • What does this tell you about the chances of avoiding all bacteria?

Day 117

Thought for the Day

All of the biggest technological inventions created by man—the airplane, the automobile, the computer—says little about his intelligence, but speaks volumes about his laziness.
—Mark Kennedy

Cool Fact

In the 1900s, before electric ignition was invented, people used burning lenses to focus the sun's rays on an object or area.

Teaser

A man is trapped in a room with two doors—the only exits. One door leads to a room made from magnifying glass, which burns anything or anyone inside by concentrating the blazing sun. Through the second door there is a fire-breathing dragon. What should the man do to escape?

Solution

He should wait until the sun sets that evening and then go through the first door.

Day 118

Thought for the Day

Science is not formal logic—it needs the free play of the mind in as great a degree as any other creative art. It is true that this is a gift which can hardly be taught, but its growth can be encouraged in those who already possess it.
—Max Born

Cool Fact

Hourglass sand timers have been used at sea since about 1400 AD because they are virtually unaffected by heat, cold, and the swinging they sometimes do as they hang from a ship's wall.

Teaser

A sundial is the instrument for measuring time that has the fewest moving parts. What is the instrument for measuring time with the most moving parts?

Solution

An hourglass.

Day 119

Thought for the Day

Science is a series of judgments, revised without ceasing.
—Pierre Émile Duclaux

Cool Fact

An element's name must be approved by the International Union of Pure and Applied Chemistry, or IUPAC, in Geneva, Switzerland.

Teaser

What does this spell?
Cobalt
Nitrogen
Germanium
Nickel
Aluminum

Solution

Congenial

The atomic symbols for these elements are Co, N, Ge, Ni, and Al.

Day 120

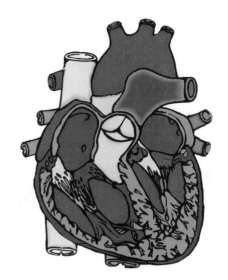

Thought for the Day

The mind likes a strange idea as little as the body likes a strange protein and resists it with similar energy. It would not perhaps be too fanciful to say that a new idea is the most quickly acting antigen known to science. If we watch ourselves honestly we shall often find that we have begun to argue against a new idea even before it has been completely stated.
—Wilfred Batten Lewis Trotter

Cool Fact

The heart is a powerful organ. As it pumps oxygen-rich blood to the rest of the body, it can generate enough pressure to squirt blood 30 feet.

Teaser

What are the 10 body parts that have only 3 letters (real names only!)?

Solution

- arm
- leg
- ear
- eye
- lip
- gum
- rib
- jaw
- toe
- hip

Day 121

Thought for the Day

There is no adequate defense, except stupidity, against the impact of a new idea.
—Percy Williams Bridgman

Cool Fact

Dolphins and bats use echolocation to find their food and get around. Echolocation is when these animals give off high-pitched sounds and interpret the echoes that bounce back.

Teaser

The Moreland Hills Marching Band taped a practice of their show behind the gym. They marched in formation, beginning and ending next to the gym wall. They played the show almost perfectly and yet when they listened to it, it was all messed up. How could that have happened?

Solution

The band members were hearing echoes. Because they were marching at the time, they were all different distances from the wall and their echoes played at different times.

Day 122

Thought for the Day

Science is piecemeal revelation.
—Oliver Wendell Holmes, Sr.

Cool Fact

Evaporation increases the power of a hurricane as it rotates in a counterclockwise direction around the calm eye. Hurricanes produce more than 74 mile-per-hour winds that, along with the heavy rain, can damage anything that gets in its way.

Teaser

Why would insurance companies be interested in sand at the bottom of the Gulf of Mexico?

Solution

The layers of sand can help tell when a hurricane will hit. There is a pattern to the layers. On average, there is a Category 5 hurricane every 3 years, although occasionally more than one can happen in a season. Insurance companies can use that theory to increase their warning for homes that are located in that area.

Day 123

Thought for the Day

Those who have an excessive faith in their theories or in their ideas are not only poorly disposed to make discoveries, but they also make very poor observations.
—Claude Bernard

Cool Fact

Mules are unique animals that not only look like the part horse-part donkey that they are, they also sound a little like both. Although they may try to bray like a donkey, the sound comes out more as a cross between the bray and a horse's whinny.

Teaser

What animal could become extinct tomorrow, but eventually thrive again in years to come?

Solution

Because they are a crossbreed between a horse and a donkey, mules could die out but, with proper breeding, thrive once again.

Day 124

Thought for the Day

The hypotheses we accept ought to explain phenomena which we have observed. But they ought to do more than this: our hypotheses ought to foretell phenomena which have not yet been observed.
—William Whewell

Cool Fact

According to the Environmental Protection Agency, many of the household cleaning products that Americans frequently use are made up of chemicals and compounds that can cause several serious illnesses including cancer, birth defects, and even the change in a person's genetic structure.

Teaser

Jimmy was washing the laundry when he spilled some bleach on the floor. He called downstairs to his wife, "Honey, could you bring me the all-purpose cleaner? I spilled some bleach and want to clean it up."

"Just wipe it up with a rag, Jimmy. If you use the cleaner, you might die," his wife responded.

Jimmy's wife was right. Why?

Solution

Most all-purpose cleaners contain ammonia. If the ammonia and the bleach were mixed together, they would create a toxic gas capable of killing instantly.

Day 125

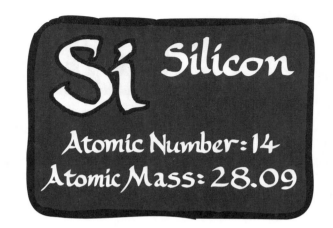

Thought for the Day

We see only what we know.
—Johann Wolfgang von Goethe

Cool Fact

Each element is assigned a chemical symbol. This symbol usually originates from its name or its Latin name. For example, silicon has the chemical symbol Si. Each element's symbol is composed of a capital letter followed by one or two lowercase letters.

Teaser

How many states have postal abbreviations that are also atomic symbols?

Solution

15

- AL Alabama (Aluminum)
- AR Arkansas (Argon)
- CA California (Calcium)
- CO Colorado (Cobalt)
- GA Georgia (Gallium)
- IN Indiana (Indium)
- LA Louisiana (Lanthanum)
- MD Maryland (Mendelevium)
- MN Minnesota (Manganese)
- MO Missouri (Molybdenum)
- MT Montana (Meitnerium)
- ND North Dakota (Neodymium)
- NE Nebraska (Neon)
- PA Pennsylvania (Protactinium)
- SC South Carolina (Scandium)

Day 126

Thought for the Day

Science increases our power in proportion as it lowers our pride.
—Claude Bernard

Cool Fact

During World War II, Winston Churchill ordered carousel owners in Britain to reopen their merry-go-rounds to boost the country's morale.

Teaser

Alex and Brenna were playing on the merry-go-round at the park. They each sat on opposite sides facing each other while they spun in a clockwise rotation. If Brenna throws a ball at Alex, will it go straight to him, to the right of him, or to the left of him?

Solution

It would go to the left of Alex because the merry-go-round will have spun slightly while the ball is in motion.

Day 127

Thought for the Day

We know very little, and yet it is astonishing that we know so much, and still more astonishing that so little knowledge can give us so much power.
—Bertrand Russell

Cool Fact

Noise-canceling headphones use the anti-noise effect by using small microphones embedded in the headset and connected to fast-acting amplifiers. The amplifier takes the noise's high-pressure wave and creates an opposite low-pressure wave, canceling out the sound.

Teaser

How is it possible for two sounds to equal silence?

Solution

If both sounds were viewed on an oscilloscope, the waves of sound 1 would be opposite of the waves of sound 2.
Sound 2's peaks and troughs appear to fill in the spaces that sound 1's waves do not. This effect is called anti-noise.

Day 128

Thought for the Day

Those who are not shocked when they first come across quantum mechanics cannot possibly have understood it.
—Niels Henrik David Bohr

Cool Fact

By using a method called optical camouflage, where the image behind the object is projected onto the object, scientists are able to achieve a kind of invisibility.

Teaser

Elizabeth's chemistry professor had just confirmed that the invisibility potion he had been working on for years finally worked. "Just one small sip and the drinker becomes completely invisible for 24 hours," said Professor Jones.

"What if it gets stolen?" Elizabeth wondered aloud to her friend, Laura. "I'll never undress in the locker room again."

"Don't worry, Elizabeth. Even if somebody did make themself invisible and sneak into the locker room, they wouldn't be able to see anything," Laura replied. Why did Laura say this?

Solution

Laura knew that if the potion really did work and could make a person invisible, it would also make him blind while he was invisible. Light is absorbed by our retinas when we see. Therefore, if a person were able to become completely invisible, the light would pass right though them. The person wouldn't be able to see anything.

Day 129

Thought for the Day

Innocence about Science is the worst crime today.
—Sir Charles Percy Snow

Cool Fact

The lower the pressure over a liquid is, the lower the boiling temperature of the liquid becomes. In other words, at sea level water boils at 100 degrees Celsius. At high elevations, where there is less air pressure, water might boil at 90 degrees Celsius.

Teaser

Because at higher altitudes you're cooking an egg at a lower temperature, the egg will take longer to cook. Now, the question is, if you were using a pressure cooker to cook an egg, would it still take longer at higher altitudes, would it take longer at lower altitudes, or would it take the same amount of time regardless of the altitude?

Solution

It would still take longer at higher altitudes because a pressure cooker doesn't control the absolute pressure inside the pot. It controls the pressure difference between the inside of the pot and the outside.

Day 130

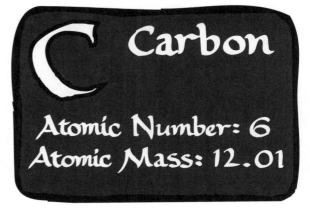

Thought for the Day

If any student comes to me and says he wants to be useful to mankind and go into research to alleviate human suffering, I advise him to go into charity instead. Research wants real egotists who seek their own pleasure and satisfaction, but find it in solving the puzzles of nature.
—Albert Szent-Györgi

Cool Fact

Carbon is part of an ever-present cycle. Over the course of millions of years, it combines with water and forms acids that dissolve rocks. The carbon is then carried to the oceans in sediments where it helps form corals and shells.

Teaser

What element is this?
Carbon
Argon
Boron
Oxygen
Nitrogen

Solution

Carbon
Carbon (C), Argon (Ar), Boron (B), Oxygen (O), Nitrogen (N)

Day 131

Thought for the Day

Happy is he who gets to know the reasons for things.
—Virgil

Cool Fact

Stopwatches, originally called chronographs, were invented by a Frenchman in 1821. It consisted of a write-on dial with a small, attached pen that was attached to the index (the face of the watch). The length of the arc of the circle displayed the time that had passed. The index stayed still while the dial moved, with the pen marking the time that passed right on the dial.

Activity

Human Stopwatch

This activity will help your students see how good they are at estimating time.

Materials:
•   One stopwatch for every pair of students.

Procedures:
1. Group students in pairs.
2. One person should hold the stopwatch and the other should estimate time.
3. Have the person with the stopwatch start the timer and say, "Go."
4. When his or her partner thinks a minute has passed, the student should say "Stop."
5. Partners should take turns several times to see if they can improve their estimation times with practice.

Day 132

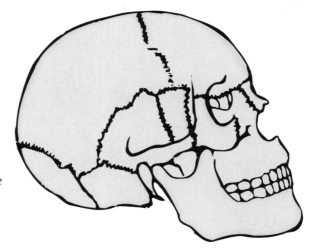

Thought for the Day

The joy of discovery is certainly the liveliest that the mind of man can ever feel.
—Claude Bernard

Cool Fact

Bone conduction is a type of normal hearing in which sound waves are conveyed to the inner ear, causing the bones of the skull to vibrate. Thus, the auditory canal and the middle ear are bypassed.

Activity

Noisy Class

This activity will demonstrate how people identify sounds when their sight is compromised.

Materials:
*   objects to make noise with, such as blocks, stones, coins, a glass, empty can, or pen
*   blindfold
*   earplugs

Procedures:
1. Blindfold one of the students and have him or her sit in the middle of the room while the other students sit at various locations around the room. Give the students different objects to make noise with, but only do so after the student has been blindfolded (so he or she can't see the objects). Tell the students to be as quiet as possible with their objects.
2. Have the blindfolded student place an earplug in one ear.
3. Randomly, and silently, point to students one at a time to make a sound with their object while the blindfolded student points in the direction of the sound and tries to identify it.

4. Repeat several times with several different students in the center, recording how many times students correctly identify the sound and the location.

5. Try it with a few more students, but this time without them plugging one of their ears. What is the difference?

6. Ask the class to think about and discuss the following questions:
   - What sounds were easiest to identify?
   - Which were hardest?
   - Does this tell you anything about the way we hear and the sounds we expect to hear?
   - What are some things you can do to improve your hearing or listening ability?

Day 133

Thought for the Day

Truth in science can be defined as the working hypothesis best suited to open the way to the next better one.
—Konrad Lorenz

Cool Fact

Humphry Davy, an English scientist, experimented with electricity in 1809. He connected wires and a piece of carbon to a battery, causing the carbon to glow and thus creating the first electric light.

Teaser

There are three different light switches on the wall, but only one does anything: It turns on the light downstairs. From where you are standing, you are unable to see the light, and it makes no sound when switched on. If you can only go downstairs to check for a light one time, how can you determine which switch is the correct one?

Solution

Flip any switch you want and let the bulb warm for several minutes. Flip that same switch off, flip another one on, and go downstairs to check the light. If it's off and hot, it was the first switch you flipped. If it's on, it is the switch you just flipped. Finally, if it's cold and off, it was the one you didn't flip.

Day 134

Thought for the Day

This only is certain, that there is nothing certain; and nothing more miserable and yet more arrogant than man.
—Pliny

Cool Fact

Thomas Edison worked long and hard to improve the longevity and glow of the light bulb. He used an invention by Herman Sprengel—a vacuum pump—to create an oxygen-free environment within a bulb, allowing the carbon filament to glow for up to 40 hours.

Activity

Homemade Light Bulb

This activity will demonstrate a simple homemade light bulb prototype.

Materials (for teacher to use in demonstration):
*   one small jar
*   cork stopper for a lid
*   3 feet of shielded copper wire
*   one 6-volt battery
*   thin iron wire

Procedures:
1. Cut the copper wire in half.
2. Poke one end of each half of the copper wire through the cork stopper.
3. Connect the iron wire from one end of the copper wire to the other.
4. Place the stopper tightly on the jar.
5. Attach one side of each half of the copper wire to the positive and negative nubs of the 6-volt battery.

6. Once the battery is attached and the charge runs through the wires, students should see a light glow—just like the first electric lights created!

7. Ask your students why they think this happened. What caused the iron to glow? (The electrical charge running through it.) How does putting it in a vacuum like Edison did increase the length of the glow? (The charge can glow longer as oxygen isn't present to interfere.)

Day 135

Thought for the Day

True science teaches us to doubt and, in ignorance, to refrain.
—Claude Bernard

Cool Fact

Near the equator, the length of the day is nearly the same as that of the night. Daylight Savings Time does not benefit countries in the tropics, so they do not change their clocks like the rest of the world.

Teaser

Patty and Jo were identical twins born in Seattle in 1973. Patty was born before Jo, but according to their birth certificates, Jo was older than Patty. How come?

Solution

Patty and Jo were born in the fall on the day that the clocks are set back one hour. Patty was born at 1:45 a.m. Jo was born 30 minutes later. Because the clocks were set back at 2 a.m., Jo's official time of birth was 1:15 a.m.

Day 136

Thought for the Day

The beginning of wisdom is found in doubting; by doubting we come to the question, and by seeking we may come upon the truth.
—Pierre Abelard

Cool Fact

The Single-Comb White Leghorn chicken is the variety responsible for laying the majority of the eggs Americans eat.

Teaser

How can you use a 7-minute hourglass and an 11-minute hourglass to boil an egg for exactly 15 minutes?

Solution

Before you put the egg in the boiling water, flip over both hourglasses. When the time runs out of the 7-minute hourglass, put the egg in the water—there will be 4 minutes left on the 11-minute hourglass. When the 11-minute hourglass runs out, flip it again, boiling the egg another 11 minutes, for a total of 15 minutes.

Day 137

Thought for the Day

The sun, with all those planets revolving around it and dependent upon it, can still ripen a bunch of grapes as if it has nothing else in the universe to do.
—Galileo

Cool Fact

When looking to improve gas mileage, some drivers need only to examine their driving habits. Aggressive driving—like quick acceleration, speeding, and braking often—can increase your gas usage by up to 33% at highway speeds and 5% at city speeds.

Teaser

Which gives a car better mileage: cold gasoline or warm gasoline?

Solution

Cold gasoline will give better gas mileage because it contains more molecules. Like most things, gasoline expands when the temperature increases.

Day 138

Thought for the Day

The process of scientific discovery is, in effect, a continual flight from wonder.
—Albert Einstein

Cool Fact

Paraffin lamps were very popular tools for lighting the Victorian home. A popular style around 1865 was the Duplex burner. This lamp had two separate wicks sitting next to each other in a clear glass chimney.

Teaser

During a power outage, Belinda realized that she was out of candles and her flashlight batteries were dead. All she had was an old paraffin lamp that had very little paraffin left inside. In fact, the paraffin was so low it didn't even reach the wick. How could she use the lamp?

Solution

She could pour water into the lamp, causing the paraffin to float until it reached the wick. Then, she could use the lamp until the paraffin ran out.

Day 139

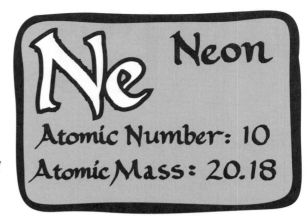

Thought for the Day

Research is to see what everybody else has seen, and to think what nobody else has thought.
—Albert Szent-Györgi

Cool Fact

Neon is a rare element found in a gaseous form, and only in about 1 part per 65,000 parts of air.

Teaser

What element is this?
Neon
Oxygen
Nitrogen

Solution

Neon
Neon (Ne), Oxygen (O), Nitrogen (N)

Day 140

Thought for the Day

Scientific principles and laws do not lie on the surface of nature. They are hidden, and must be wrested from nature by an active and elaborate technique of inquiry.
—John Dewey

Cool Fact

The Arctic ice cap consists of 6.5–10 feet of thick, floating sea ice. In the colder months of the year, the surface area of the ice cap is larger than the United States, but it shrinks to half that size during the warmer months.

Teaser

"It should have been one of the most exciting experiences of my life. I was on a once-in-a-lifetime expedition to the North Pole, but have nothing to show for it. I caught a cold my third day out there and couldn't hold the camera straight for all my sneezing and coughing. Not to mention the watery eyes—I couldn't even focus when I looked through the view finder," Nancy told Trevor.

"Nice try, Nancy. What's the real reason you don't have any pictures from your expedition—if you really went on one at all?" Trevor said.

How did Trevor know Nancy was lying?

Solution

Trevor knew that Nancy couldn't have caught a cold at the North Pole (if she went at all), because cold viruses can't survive in the extreme cold.

Day 141

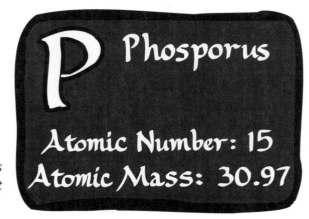

Thought for the Day

More than ever, the creation of the ridiculous is almost impossible because of the competition it receives from reality.
—Robert A. Baker

Cool Fact

Phosphorus can be found in three different forms. White phosphorus is a clear, colorless, soft, waxy solid and can give off a green glow in the dark. Red phosphorus is a brownish-red powder. Black phosphorus is graphite-like, flaky, and metallic.

Teaser

What element is this?
Phosphorus
Hydrogen
Oxygen
Sulphur
Phosphorus
Hydrogen
Oxygen
Ruthenium
Sulphur

Solution

Phosphorus
Phosphorus (P), Hydrogen (H), Oxygen (O), Sulphur (S), Phosphorus (P), Hydrogen (H), Oxygen (O), Ruthenium (Ru), Sulphur (S)

Day 142

Thought for the Day

In all science, error precedes the truth, and it is better it should go first than last.
—Hugh Walpole

Cool Fact

Trying to find ways to write secret messages in invisible ink has long been a favorite pastime. The easiest way is to find a heat-sensitive liquid and let it dry completely. Lemon juice, onion juice, milk, and vinegar are all liquids that will work. When it's time to reveal the secret message, the recipient need only to hold the paper over a candle or light bulb.

Teaser

Faith is planning a practical joke to pull on her sister, Allie. Faith came up with a way to write her notes in invisible ink, that way if Allie came across them before she was done, all Allie would see was a blank sheet of paper. When Faith was ready to put her plan into action, she would be able to read the notes easily. How?

Solution

Faith wrote her notes in lemon juice, so when she was ready, all she needed to do was hold her notes over a flame. The dried juice would become a reddish brown color when heated, clearly revealing her words.

Day 143

Thought for the Day

*When we try to pick out anything by itself, we find it
is tied to everything else in the universe.*
—John Muir

Cool Fact

Silicon is a nonmetallic element that can sometimes be found in
a crystalline form, much like a diamond.

Teaser

What element is this?
Silicon
Lithium
Carbon
Oxygen
Nitrogen

Solution

Silicon
Silicon (Si), Lithium (Li), Carbon (C), Oxygen (O), Nitrogen
(N)

Day 144

Thought for the Day

Men are probably nearer the central truth in their superstitions than in their science.
—Quinn David Thoreau

Cool Fact

Mosquitoes find new hosts by observing movement, detecting infrared radiation emitted by warm bodies, and by chemical signals. They are attracted to carbon dioxide and lactic acid, among other chemicals.

Teaser

Why don't you feel or see a mosquito bite until after it starts itching?

Solution

The mosquito bites by inserting her lancets into the capillary beds beneath the skin, and drinks by lubricating her mouth with saliva. The saliva acts as an anesthetic and contains an anticoagulant that causes an allergic reaction in humans—hence the bump and redness.

Day 145

Thought for the Day

I am compelled to fear that science will be used to promote the power of dominant groups rather than to make men happy.
—Bertrand Russell

Cool Fact

Eyes, which can detect more than 200 separate colors, can process an amazing 36,000 pieces of information every hour.

Teaser

Candace is an expert collector. She travels the world looking for and negotiating for unique pieces of artwork. Wherever she goes, regardless of the light, she insists on wearing dark sunglasses. Why?

Solution

Candace knows that the pupils of your eyes give clues as to your emotions. For a seller to know she really wanted something, all he would have to do is look into her eyes.

Day 146

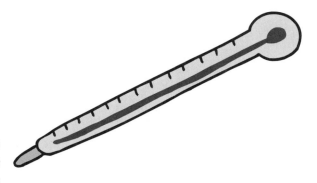

Thought for the Day

Physics is mathematical not because we know so much about the physical world, but because we know so little; it is only its mathematical properties that we can discover.
—Bertrand Russell

Cool Fact

Although several inventors created a version of early thermometers, or thermoscopes, at around the same time, Santorio Santorio was the first to put a numerical scale on it.

Teaser

"The temperature of this solution is minus 40 degrees," Professor Palmer told her assistant, who was recording observations for her.

"Celsius or Fahrenheit?" her assistant asked.

"It doesn't matter," Professor Palmer replied.

Why didn't it matter?

Solution

At minus 40 degrees (and only minus 40) the temperature is the same at Fahrenheit and Celsius.

Day 147

Thought for the Day

Science, like life, feeds on its own decay. New facts burst old rules; then newly divined conceptions bind old and new together into a reconciling law.
—William James

Cool Fact

Overall, there is a 51% chance a couple will have a boy and a 49% chance they will have a girl. However, with subsequent pregnancies, the odds go up that they will continue having the same gender.

Teaser

Mr. and Mrs. Vale have five children. Half of them are girls. How is this possible?

Solution

The other half are girls, too.

Day 148

Thought for the Day

For every fact there is an infinity of hypotheses.
—Robert M. Pirsig

Cool Fact

Dry ice can stay 15 times cooler than wet ice, making it ideal for keeping large quantities of food or beverages cold for long periods of time.

Teaser

Harry offered Shelly a glass of lemonade. "I'd love one, especially if it is really cold," Shelly said.

Harry brought over two glasses and a filled ice bucket. Using ice tongs, he dropped a small ice cube in each glass of lemonade. Shelly took a sip of hers, and noted it wasn't very cold.

"Give it a minute," Harry said. The lemonade in each glass appeared to be boiling. When the ice cube melted, the boiling stopped and the lemonade was super cold. What happened?

Solution

Harry dropped dry ice in the lemonade. It gave the appearance that it was boiling while it melted and quickly cooled the drinks.

Day 149

Thought for the Day

When truth is evident, it is impossible for parties and factions to rise. There never has been a dispute as to whether there is daylight at noon.
—François-Marie Arouet de Voltaire

Cool Fact

In the Sangre de Cristo Mountains, in southern Colorado, America's tallest sand dunes rise more than 700 feet high. Over the years, wind has shaped these dunes. This geologic wonderland, containing 39 square miles of dunes, became a national monument in 1932.

Activity

Sand Dunes

This activity will demonstrate how sand dunes are formed and some of the circumstances that affect their formation.

Materials (for each group):
- hair dryer
- 2 flat pans
- small grass clumps
- small stones
- clean sand

Procedures:
1. Have students label the pans A and B.
2. Students should fill them with sand.
3. Have them arrange stones and grass in different areas of pan B.
4. Ask your students to hold their hairdryer at a 45-degree angle, point it at pan A and blow for one minute.
5. Have them record all of their observations, and then repeat this process with pan B.
6. Have them draw a sketch of each pan after one minute of blowing.

7. Then, ask them to level each pan and repeat the above steps, blowing for 3 minutes.

8. Talk about their findings (and have them help sweep up the sand on the floor!).

9. Ask students why the sand formed into such varying patterns. (The makeup of the landscape has an impact on what the land does.)

Day 150

Thought for the Day

Every sentence I utter must be understood not as an affirmation, but as a question.
—Niels Henrik David Bohr

Cool Fact

Being hygroscopic, or able to absorb liquid well, salt is sometimes spread on the floors of barns to hold in the moisture and keep the dust down.

Teaser

Abby helped her father carry bags of salt to sell at the market each day. The bags were heavy and she hated the job. Whenever she complained, her father told her that everybody had a job to do in a family and this was hers. One day, she tripped while walking and fell into the roadside creek. When she stood up, she noticed that the salt bags were lighter. (Some of the salt had dissolved, which helped lighten her load.) Each day after that, she purposely fell into the creek, making her bags lighter, and annoying her father as she brought him bag after bag of useless salt.

Her father, after several days of receiving ruined salt, prepared special salt bags for her to carry. When Abby fell into the water with these, she learned her lesson immediately and apologized to her father. What did he do?

Solution

He filled her bags with sand, making them much heavier when they became waterlogged.

Day 151

Thought for the Day

Metaphysics is a dark ocean without shores or lighthouse, strewn with many a philosophic wreck.
—Immanuel Kant

Cool Fact

In ancient Greece, slaves were traded for salt, which is where the saying, "not worth his salt" comes from.

Teaser

It comes from water, but makes you thirsty.
It corrodes metal, but preserves food.
It is hard, yet softens water.
It is a mineral, but you eat it.
What is it?

Solution

Salt

Day 152

Thought for the Day

Scientists are explorers. Philosophers are tourists.
—Richard Feynman

Cool Fact

The "Game of Nim" is a mathematically perfect game. To win the game every time, you use a simple system—simply hit the key numbers and you can't lose.

Teaser

Quinn and Rachel are going to play a game. Quinn explains, "You and I will take turns saying numbers. The first person will say a number between 1 and 10. Then the other person will say a number that is at least one higher than that number, and at most 10 higher. For example, if I say 3, you can say 4, 5, 6, 7, 8, 9, 10, 11, 12, or 13. Next, I say a number that is between 1 and 10 higher than the number you just said. We will keep going back and forth in this way until one of us says the number 50. That person wins. I'll start."

"Not so fast!" says Rachel. "I want to win, so I will start."

What number should Rachel say to start?

Solution

Rachel should start with 6.
The series of numbers she should say is 6, 17, 28, 39, and 50.

Day 153

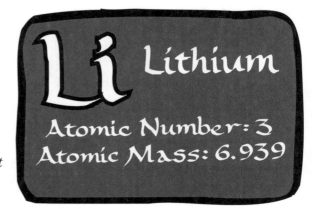

Thought for the Day

If your experiment needs statistics, then you ought to have done a better experiment.
—Ernest Rutherford

Cool Fact

Lithium is the lightest of all metals, which is ironic because its name comes from the Greek word *lithos*, which means stone.

Teaser

What does this spell?
Lithium
Oxygen
Nitrogen

Solution

LiON
Lithium (Li), Oxygen (O), Nitrogen (N)

Day 154

Thought for the Day

A great pleasure in life is doing what people say you cannot do.
—Walter Bagehot

Cool Fact

The genes that decide a person's hair color, called *melanocytes*, are present before birth. These cells can distinguish between black, brown, and red. Depending on the percentage of each type of cell, the person will have blonde, brown, red, or black hair.

Teaser

You are visiting a new town and need a haircut. There are only two barbers in town. You visit each shop. One is disorganized and messy and the barber has a horrible haircut. The other one is neat and tidy and the barber has a wonderful haircut. Which barber would you choose and why?

Solution

Go to the barber with the disorganized shop. He probably gave the neat barber his beautiful haircut.

Day 155

Thought for the Day

A great frustration in life is discovering that sometimes those who say something can't be done turn out to be right.
—Donald Simanek

Cool Fact

Birthday parties started in Europe a long time ago because people though that evil spirits were particularly attracted to people on their birthdays. In an attempt to protect them from harm, friends and family would to come to the birthday person and bring good thoughts and wishes. Giving gifts brought even more good cheer to ward off the evil spirits.

Teaser

The day before yesterday Amy was 13 years old. Next year she will be 16. How is this possible?

Solution

Her birthday is on December 31. If today is January 1, then the day before yesterday, she was 13, yesterday she turned 14, this year she'll turn 15, and next year she'll turn 16.

Day 156

Thought for the Day

I do not know what I may appear to the world; but to myself I seem to have been only like a boy playing on the seashore, and diverting myself in now and then finding of a smoother pebble or a prettier shell than ordinary, whilst the great ocean of truth lay all undiscovered before me.
—Sir Isaac Newton

Cool Fact

A hollow rock with fat-soaked moss was ignited more than 70,000 years ago to form the first lamp.

Teaser

The Kehres family had a European exchange student visiting them. On the night before he was to leave their home in Florida, he presented them with a beautiful lamp that he said had been in his family for years. "It's a European antique," he claimed. "And I want you to have it." He plugged it in to show the family how it worked.

Later, when the exchange student had gone to bed, Chris said to his father, "You know, it's a nice lamp and all, but it's not from Europe."

How did he know?

Solution

If it had been from Europe, it would not have worked in American outlets. He couldn't have plugged it in.

Day 157

Thought for the Day

Genius is one percent inspiration and ninety-nine percent perspiration.
—Thomas Alva Edison

Cool Fact

The post office has an annual operating revenue of nearly $70 billion and employs more than 700,000 career employees who communicate with each other on the world's largest intranet.

Teaser

A man has just finished painting his house and needs something. He goes to a hardware store and asks for help in finding what he needs. The clerk shows him where the objects are and tells him that they cost $1 each. The man says: "I'm taking 2282, so here's $4." What did he buy?

Solution

Numbers to put on his house to display his address.

Day 158

Thought for the Day

Most institutions demand unqualified faith; but the institution of science makes skepticism a virtue.
—Robert K. Merton

Cool Fact

Dry ice has the approximate temperature of -109.3 degrees Fahrenheit, making it very dangerous to handle. If dry ice comes into contact with the skin, it will cause a severe burn-like injury.

Teaser

David challenged Cara to lift an ice cube out of a glass of water with a string. He told her she couldn't touch the ice cube or tie any knots in the string. She did it easily, using only something normally found on the dinner table. How did she do this?

Solution

First, she dipped the string in the water, then laid a part of it over the top of the ice cube. She then sprinkled some salt on the top of the ice cube. The ice melted a little, but stopped when she stopped pouring the salt. The water that formed on the top of the cube refroze, embedding the string and making it easy to lift.

Day 159

Thought for the Day

The whole history of physics proves that a new discovery is quite likely lurking at the next decimal place.
—F. K. Richtmeyer

Cool Fact

Reuben H. Donnelly is credited with creating the first business yellow pages in 1886. This phone book was categorized by type of business and service.

Teaser

Cheryl held up a yellow pages phone book and announced to her family that she would amaze them by tearing the book in half with her bare hands. She took a deep breath and tore it easily. (She did not tear it down the middle of the spine.)

How did she do this?

Solution

Beforehand, she baked the phone book in the oven to make it brittle and easy to tear. The oven is turned on to a low setting, and the book is essentially being dried out. It may take several hours to do this, depending on the size of the book.

Day 160

Thought for the Day

The task of asking nonliving matter to speak and the responsibility for interpreting its reply is that of physics.
—J. T. Fraser

Cool Fact

The amount of cloud cover is measured in oktas on a scale from 0 to 8. Eight oktas means the sky is totally covered, as compared to 0 oktas, which means that it is totally clear.

Teaser

What is the highest number that can be written with only four letters?

Solution

A mole: 602,000,000,000,000,000,000,000. A mole is a unit that measures a specific amount of substance.

Day 161

Thought for the Day

The quantum is that embarrassing little piece of thread that always hangs from the sweater of space-time. Pull it and the whole thing unravels.
—Fred Alan Wolfe

Cool Fact

The most familiar and widely used solvent is water, but acetone, alcohol, and turpentine are also very common.

Teaser

Julie told Denny that she had a vial of a special solvent that would dissolve any substance it touched.

Denny knew she was lying. How?

Solution

It hadn't dissolved the vial.

Day 162

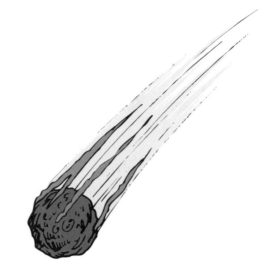

Thought for the Day

The doubter is a true man of science; he doubts only himself and his interpretations, but he believes in science.
—Claude Bernard

Cool Fact

Although the outside, or fusion crust, of a meteorite can be hot immediately after impact, its inside stays completely frozen.

Teaser

A man claiming to be an astronomer tried to join the local astronomy club. Bragging, he said, "Why, just the other day I saw a large meteorite flying through the sky."

The astronomers in the club, knowing he was not an astronomer, suggested he try another club.

How did they know?

Solution

A meteorite is a meteor that has landed on a planet. Any astronomer would know that!

Day 163

Thought for the Day

In physics, you don't have to go around making trouble for yourself—nature does it for you.
—Frank Wilczek

Cool Fact

Venus is about the same size as the Earth, but is covered with clouds of carbon dioxide and sulfur.

Teaser

Which is longer: a year or a day on Venus?

Solution

A day. It takes Venus 243 Earth days to rotate on its axis, but it takes only 225 Earth days to go around the sun.

Day 164

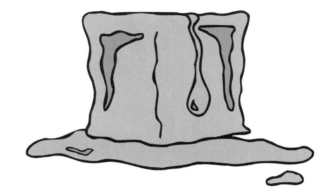

Thought for the Day

Science without conscience is the soul's perdition.
—François Rabelais

Cool Fact

Natural occurrences that can weaken ice on lakes, streams, and ponds are water-level fluctuations and the actions of birds and fish. For example, schools of carp create thin ice spots or even open water by congregating in one location while circulating the water with their fins.

Teaser

Which liquid is denser in its liquid form than its solid form?

Solution

Water, which is why ice floats when placed in a glass of water.

Day 165

Thought for the Day

Even if the open windows of science at first make us shiver after the cozy indoor warmth of traditional humanizing myths, in the end the fresh air brings vigor, and the great spaces have a splendor of their own.
—Bertrand Russell

Cool Fact

Birds have very fragile bones that do not fossilize as readily as bones of mammals and reptiles. As a consequence, we know a lot less about the history of birds than we know about mammals and reptiles.

Teaser

Scientists had been thinking about sending birds up to space to study them in zero gravity, but realized that, despite providing them with plenty of fresh food and drinking water, they would die. Why?

Solution

Although humans can swallow without gravity, birds cannot.

Day 166

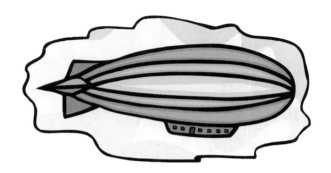

Thought for the Day

Ethics and Science need to shake hands.
—Richard Clarke Cabot

Cool Fact

Blimps and balloons that use helium for flotation are usually very large because helium weighs only slightly less than the air. When dealing with such small weight differences, the extra room to collect more helium makes a big difference.

Teaser

A helium balloon is tied to the floor of the car. The windows are closed and the air conditioning is off, so there is no breeze to displace the balloon. If the car makes a sharp turn, what will the balloon do?

Solution

Due to buoyancy, the helium balloon on the string will tend to move in the direction opposite the gravitational field existing in the car. So, when the car turns the corner, the balloon will deflect toward the inside of the turn.

Day 167

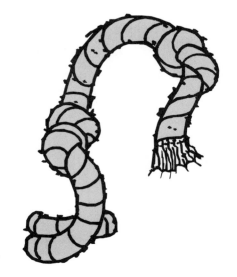

Thought for the Day

Science is all those things which are confirmed to such a degree that it would be unreasonable to withhold one's provisional consent.
—Stephen Jay Gould

Cool Fact

Because nylon "remembers" its original shape and length, it can snap back, making it one of the strongest rope types used today.

Teaser

How can you tie a knot in a length of rope while holding an end in each hand and without letting go of either end?

Solution

Cross your arms before grabbing the ends of the rope, then uncross your arms, leaving a knot in the rope.

Day 168

Thought for the Day

Science is a first-rate piece of furniture for a man's upper chamber, if he has common sense on the ground floor.
—Oliver Wendell Holmes, Sr.

Cool Fact

Hard water contains a lot of calcium and magnesium, and is not well-suited for household water usage.

Teaser

I have a cup of water with an ice cube floating in it. When the ice melts, will I have more or less water in my cup?

Solution

The same amount. Whether the water is frozen (ice cube) or liquid, it is still water.

Day 169

Thought for the Day

The whole of science is nothing more than a refinement of everyday thinking.
—Albert Einstein

Cool Fact

Of all the water on Earth, only 2.5% is fresh water. Accessible fresh water is either groundwater (0.5%), or water in lakes, streams, rivers, and the like (0.01%). The rest of the freshwater on Earth is tied up in glaciers and ice caps.

Teaser

If I dropped one weight into a bucket of 40-degree Fahrenheit water and one into a bucket of 30-degree Fahrenheit water, which would hit the bottom first?

Solution

The weight dropped into the 40-degree bucket. The water in the 30-degree bucket is frozen.

Day 170

Thought for the Day

Research is the process of going up alleys to see if they are blind.
—Marston Bates

Cool Fact	If all of the world's water were fit into a gallon jug, the fresh water available for us to use would equal only about one tablespoon.
Teaser	Ellie was playing with a tennis ball in her backyard, when the ball got away from her and rolled down into a hole. The hole was too deep for her to reach the ball and there was a slight bend at the bottom, but using something she found in the garden, she was able to get the ball easily. How did she reach the tennis ball?
Solution	She took a garden hose and filled the hole with water. The ball floated to the top.

Day 171

Thought for the Day

No problem can stand the assault of sustained thinking.
—François-Marie Arouet de Voltaire

Cool Fact

In 1911, the telephone repairman was mobile, mechanized, and well-equipped. With his tools around his waist, he carried telephones on his back, chest, and in his bicycle sack. Like today, telephone men 80 years ago were safety-minded, which in that era included wearing sleeve guards and trouser clips.

Teaser

The following group of numbers represents an 11-letter word. Can you figure out the word?
46244628466
31113211332

Solution

Imagination! Looking at a telephone, the first row of numbers is what number to look on. The second row is which letter to look at on the particular number. For example, to get the first letter of the mystery word, you go to the number 4 on the telephone and then look at the third letter listed on that number: I.

Day 172

Thought for the Day

Chance favors the prepared mind.
—Louis Pasteur

Cool Fact

Although the game of chess dates to ancient times, no one knows for sure which culture deserves credit for its conception.

Teaser

Kaylee had never won a game of chess against Meghan, so one day she bet her that she could simultaneously play two chess games with her, and either win one of the games or draw both of them. She made only one stipulation, which was that they alternate their moves on two separate chess boards and that on one board she got to play black while on the other board she got to play white. She said that she was so confident that she would win this bet that she would let Meghan play first. Meghan accepted the challenge. How was Kaylee able to win this bet?

Solution

Meghan opened with a white move on the first board. Kaylee then made the same opening move with white on the second board. Meghan made her answering black move on the second board. Kaylee then made this same answering move with black on board one. They played back and forth with Kaylee always using Meghan's moves on one board as her own moves on the other board. This meant that Meghan was playing herself and that if she won one of the games she would lose the other game, or she could draw both games. But, in no way could she win both of the games.

Day 173

Thought for the Day

Some things need to be believed to be seen.
—Guy Kawasaki

Cool Fact

Some birds use the stars and the sounds from the Earth to guide them as they migrate overnight.

Teaser

Julie, Alexander, and Sarah went bird watching. Each of them saw one bird that none of the others did. Each pair saw one bird that the third did not. And, one bird was seen by all three. Of the birds Julie saw, two were yellow. Of the birds Alexander saw, three were yellow. Of the birds Sarah saw, four were yellow. How many yellow birds were seen in all? How many non-yellow birds were seen in all?

Solution

Three birds were seen by one person each, three were seen by each unique pair (Julie-Alexander, Julie-Sarah, and Alexander-Sarah), and one was seen by all three. So, seven birds were seen in all, and each person saw a total of four. Hence, all of the birds Sarah saw were yellow. These four birds are: (1) the one Sarah saw alone, (2) the one Sarah saw with Julie, (3) the one Sarah saw with Alexander, and (4) the one all three saw together. This accounts for both of the yellow birds Julie saw, and two of the three yellow birds Alexander saw. The third yellow bird Alexander saw could not have been the one Julie and Alexander saw together, because Julie only saw two yellow birds, so the third yellow bird Alexander saw must have been the one he saw alone.

Five yellow birds were seen (the one Alexander saw, the one Sarah saw, the one Julie and Sarah saw, the one Alexander and Sarah saw, and the one all three saw). Two non-yellow birds were seen (the one Julie saw and the one Julie and Alexander saw) by the group.

Day 174

Thought for the Day

The eternal mystery of the world is its comprehensibility.
—Albert Einstein

Cool Fact

The art of weather forecasting has been around for centuries. The ancient Babylonians tried to predict short-term weather changes based on the appearance of clouds and optical phenomena such as haloes as early as 650 BC.

Teaser

John was watching television. Just after the midnight news, there was a weather forecast: "It is raining now and will rain for the next two days. However, in 72 hours it will be bright and sunny."

"Those weather reporters are always wrong!" snorted John. He was correct, but how did he know?

Solution

In 72 hours it would be midnight again, so it could not be bright and sunny.

Day 175

Thought for the Day

[Science is] an imaginative adventure of the mind seeking truth in a world of mystery.
—Sir Cyril Herman Hinshelwood

Cool Fact

Sam Heath set the record for enclosing the most people inside a single bubble (19 boys and girls) at Chessington World of Adventures outside London in 2006.

Activity

Popping Bubbles

This activity uses inquiry to allow students to draw conclusions.

Materials (for each student):
• bubble solution
• bubble wands
• various surfaces (e.g., paper, wool, desks, vinyl, wax paper)

Procedures:
1. Have your students predict what will happen when they blow their bubbles on various surfaces. (Bubbles will pop instantly on rough surfaces, but may stay around longer on wet or slick surfaces.)
2. Have them test their hypothesis by blowing several bubbles onto each of the surfaces and then record their observations.
3. Discuss their findings. Did their hypotheses turn out to be correct? What surprised them?

Day 176

Thought for the Day

In essence, science is a perpetual search for an intelligent and integrated comprehension of the world we live in.
—Cornelius Bernardus Van Neil

Cool Fact

The longest documented lifespan is that of Jeanne Calment of France who lived from 1875–1997, and died at age 122 years and 164 days.

Teaser

My grandmother is a remarkable woman. She has lived through three centuries, but she is only slightly more than 100 years old. How can this be?

She was born at the end of one century, lived through a full one, and was currently living in the beginning of the third. (Example: She was born in 1899, lived 1900–1999, and is living in 2000.)

Day 177

Thought for the Day

Science can only ascertain what is, but not what should be, and outside of its domain value judgments of all kinds remain necessary.
—Albert Einstein

Cool Fact

Bubbles always try to minimize their surface area, so if two bubbles come into contact, they will merge to share a common wall.

Teaser

If it took 5 seconds for one popper to pop, 5 seconds for two poppers to pop, 5 seconds for three poppers to pop, and 5 seconds for four poppers to pop, how many seconds would it take for 100 poppers to pop?

Solution

5 seconds. They all go at the same time!

Day 178

Thought for the Day

It would be a poor thing to be an atom in a universe without physicists, and physicists are made of atoms. A physicist is an atom's way of knowing about atoms.
—George Wald

Cool Fact

Because sharks rely on ram-ventilation—their forward swimming to push oxygen-bearing water through their mouths and over their gills—scientists believe they don't sleep.

Teaser

E. J. and Steve were out fishing in their dinghy when they saw a shark circling nearby. Whenever they tried to move the boat toward shore, the shark would slam into it, almost capsizing their boat. "Don't worry," Steve said. "Let's just wait. Eventually it will fall asleep and we can leave then."

Was Steve's advice good?

Solution

No. Sharks do not sleep like humans do.